Collaborating with Customers to Innovate

Emanuela wishes to dedicate this book to her mother, Maria Rosa
Mohan wishes to dedicate this book to his kids, Haki, Asha, Naina
and Bundev
Gianmario wishes to dedicate this book to his wife, Paola, and to his son,
Lorenzo

Collaborating with Customers to Innovate

Conceiving and Marketing Products in the Networking Age

Emanuela Prandelli

Associate Professor of Management, Bocconi University, Italy

Mohanbir Sawhney

McCormick Tribune Professor of Marketing, Northwestern University, USA

Gianmario Verona

Professor of Management, Bocconi University, Italy

Edward Elgar
Cheltenham, UK • Northampton, MA, USA

Published by
Edward Elgar Publishing Limited
The Lypiatts
15 Lansdown Road
Cheltenham
Glos GL50 2JA
UK

Edward Elgar Publishing, Inc.
William Pratt House
9 Dewey Court
Northampton
Massachusetts 01060
USA

A catalogue record for this book
is available from the British Library

Library of Congress Control Number: 2008927975

ISBN 978 1 84720 373 1 (cased)

Printed and bound in Great Britain by MPG Books Ltd, Bodmin, Cornwall

Contents

Figures

Tables

Notes on the authors

Emanuela Prandelli is Associate Professor of Management at Università Bocconi and Senior Lecturer at the SDA Bocconi School of Management. She holds a PhD in Management and served as a research assistant at St. Gallen University in 1998, and at the Research Center on Technology, Innovation, and eCommerce of the Kellogg School of Management, Northwestern University in 1999, where she was also Visiting Professor in 2001. Her research focuses on collaborative marketing, virtual communities of consumption, the study of e-business and the process of innovation. She has published several articles in leading international journals such as *California Management Review*, *Organization Studies*, the *Journal of Interactive Marketing*, *MIT Sloan Management Review* and the *European Management Journal*. She won the 2001 Accenture Award for the best paper published in *California Management Review* in 2000.

Mohanbir Sawhney is the McCormick Tribune Professor of Technology and the Director, Center for Research in Technology and Innovation at the Kellogg School of Management, Northwestern University. He holds a PhD in Marketing from the Wharton School of the University of Pennsylvania. His research interests include collaborative marketing with customers, information technology and business agility, customer-centric organization design, organic growth and business innovation. He has published several influential articles in leading journals such as *California Management Review*, *Harvard Business Review*, the *Journal of Interactive Marketing*, *Management Science*, *Marketing Science*, *MIT Sloan Management Review* and the *Journal of the Academy of Marketing Science*. He has won several awards for his research and teaching, most recently the Sidney Levy Award for Excellence in Teaching at the Kellogg School in 2006. This is his fifth book.

Gianmario Verona is Professor of Management at Università Bocconi and is currently Visiting Professor at the Tuck School of Business at Dartmouth College. He is Associate Director of the PhD in Business Administration and Management at Bocconi and Senior Lecturer at the SDA Bocconi School of Management. He holds a PhD in Management and was a research assistant at the Sloan School of Management at the Massachusetts

Institute of Technology (1997–98). His research interests include the knowledge-based view of the firm with particular focus on exploration strategies and the impact of market knowledge on a firm's innovation process. His articles have been published in leading journals, including the *Academy of Management Review, Organization Studies, Industrial and Corporate Change, MIT Sloan Management Review, California Management Review* and the *Journal of Interactive Marketing*.

Acknowledgments

This book is the result of seven years' cooperation between the three of us on the topic of collaborative and open innovation. The book would have not been possible without the contribution of several firms and the unique support that many colleagues gave us, with both their time and thoughts. In particular, we benefited tremendously from our conversations with the following people, each of whom generously shared their insights on various topics: Miguel Ares (Diesel), Dr Alp Bingham (Eli Lilly), Guido Gerlotti (IBM.COM), Larry Huston (formerly at P&G), Federico Minoli, Patrizia Cianetti and Luisa Ercoli (Ducati Motor Company), and Peter Steinlauf and Jeremy Anwyl (Edmunds.com).

Emanuela and Gianmario would like to acknowledge their gratitude to Salvio Vicari and Enrico Valdani for their valuable encouragement and deep interest in this project and, more generally, for promoting their research activity on innovation management at Università Bocconi. They also want to thank Alfonso Gambardella for sharing relevant insights about open innovation and markets for technology. They would also like to express their appreciation to Paola Cillo and Deborah Raccagni for their systematic and generous comments on a previous version of the manuscript. Finally, they are grateful to the Università Bocconi and in particular to Associate Dean Lorenzo Peccati for partially funding this project.

Emanuela would like to express her deep gratitude to her husband Michele, for his patience, enthusiasm, and, above all, for his love and continuous support. This makes a tremendous difference both in her work and in her life. Emanuela would also like to thank her little daughters, Francesca and Federica, for the extraordinary joy they bring her every single day. She finally thanks Ariela and Paola, for their unique friendship and help.

Mohan would like to thank his mother, Kuldeep Sawhney, for her unwavering support through good and bad times, and his wife, Parminder, for being a loud cheerleader.

Gianmario would like to thank his father, Mario, and his mother, Rita, for their unique and generous support in every single moment of his life.

Introduction

Anything that won't sell, I don't want to invent
Thomas Edison

In a tough business environment, innovation is the only route to gaining and sustaining competitive advantage. In the past few years, governments, journalists, CEOs and academicians have embraced innovation as the new Holy Grail for the future development of countries, industries and firms. As students of innovation for several years, we are heartened by the widespread appeal of innovation as a subject for study and practice. At the same time, we are concerned that the substance is getting lost in the hype surrounding the subject, and anecdotal success stories are becoming a substitute for serious research on innovation. Indeed, innovation is difficult to grasp at a conceptual level, and it is even more difficult to implement as a methodical and repeatable process. So when we decided to write this book, we chose to address the topic of innovation from two specific angles.

First, we limit our focus to the role that customers are beginning to play in innovation. We do not attempt to provide a complete treatment of the broad and complex subject of innovation theory and management. Instead, our book seeks to help managers understand how their firms can collaborate with customers at all stages of the innovation process. Customers are the only reason that a firm exists. Therefore, it seems logical to us that they should be the most valuable contributors to the firm's innovation efforts. However, many issues get in the way of collaborative innovation with customers, including the 'not invented here' syndrome of research and development (R&D) labs, functional and business unit silos, poor quality of market research tools, and the lack of cost-effective ways to conduct a dialogue with customers. We believe that many of these barriers can be overcome by the possibilities that digital networks open up for customer collaboration.

Second, and as a direct consequence, we focus on the tools and technologies that enable co-creation as firms engage customers in innovation activities. We examine the enabling role of information and communication technologies (ICTs), and more specifically, the Internet, in collaborative innovation. The Internet is a powerful force for transformation of innovation, and we show how firms can leverage the network to take co-creation to the next level. We believe that the Internet and more generally ICTs have distinctive characteristics that can turbo-charge innovation, and that these characteristics have not been studied adequately in innovation and marketing textbooks.

The thesis of our book is simple – customers offer valuable creativity and expertise that can be harnessed in digital environments to enhance the effectiveness of the new product development process. The Internet is the source of the problem that firms face today in innovation – the life cycle of innovative products is shrinking in a network-enabled world where information is transparent, competitors are just one click away, and products get commoditized rapidly. However, the Internet also provides the solution – enabling new forms of value creation with customers and an efficient way to harness distributed competences. Specifically, we highlight the role that digital environments play in allowing firms to engage customers in product design and testing. We define the management of these processes as 'collaborative innovation'.

We provide a comprehensive review of technology-based tools for marketing interaction and then show how these tools can be mapped to each stage of the collaborative innovation process. We also extend our scope beyond the firm, to study how collaborative innovation is part of the broader phenomenon of distributed innovation – that is, the phenomenon of extending innovation beyond a firm's boundaries. Indeed, at the network level, innovation is empowered not only by customer collaboration, but also by 'communities of creation', virtual knowledge brokering and open-source systems. We provide actionable recommendations for putting collaborative innovation and distributed innovation to work in each chapter.

We hope that our book will enrich an important debate in the academy about 'innovating innovation' as we come to grips with the possibilities of the networked digital world we live in. And we hope that managers can glean actionable and insightful ideas on how they can master the innovation challenge by partnering with customers with the powerful tools they now have at their command.

1. An increasing need for innovation

1.1 INTRODUCTION

Almost a century ago, Joseph Schumpeter (1991), a heterodox Austrian economist, argued that economics needs to do more than simply be the science that studies the allocation of scarce resources. If this were the case, the economic problems would simply be a matter of algorithms and equations. Schumpeter believed that economics should focus on the dynamics of change stimulated by innovation. Innovation promotes growth and generates imitation. In so doing, it causes repeated cycles where equilibria are formed and then destroyed. Economics has, in its very nature, the force that sustains but also destroys. Therefore, it is a science that must also study innovation, progress and the evolution of social systems. As Schumpeter points out, the different forms of innovation, including new products, new processes, organizational innovations and new kinds of markets, represent a significant driver of capitalist systems and the economies of different countries.

Innovation does not happen by serendipity or chance. It is a systematic process that needs to be managed. Indeed, Schumpeter (1943), in highlighting the strategic and organizational implications of innovation, suggested that innovation can be a managerial process in a large enterprise. Large firms can systematically create innovation through their research and development (R&D) efforts, and they can harness the profits generated by innovations to protect themselves from the competitive forces of their markets.

While Schumpeter understood the principal dynamics of innovation at the industrial level, as well as the entrepreneurial and managerial drive behind innovation, he could only catch a glimpse of the strong inertia in organizations that attempt to create innovations. After all, innovation involves the creation of something new, so it is a process that requires learning. But too often, firms are plagued with learning disabilities that are created by the very competences that sustain them. To promote innovation, firms need to embrace an evolutionary approach that can transform their competences over time.

In this chapter, we illustrate how firms can deal with the challenge of sustaining innovation in dynamic and uncertain environments, and how they can enhance their capacity for innovation by leveraging distributed innovation.[1] We base our discussion on the extensive literature on innovation from economists and management scholars, as well as the considerable body of empirical research on innovation (see for detailed reviews: Brown and Eisenhardt, 1995; Verona, 1999; Krishnan and Ulrich, 2001; Hauser et al., 2007). This research has developed valuable models and frameworks for creating, developing, launching and marketing innovative products.

We begin by outlining the risks behind innovation and the organizational structures that firms have adopted in managing innovations (Section 1.2). Next, we focus on the strategic orientations that move companies towards innovation in more complex environmental contexts (Section 1.3). Finally, we discuss why firms collaborate with several partners and distribute innovative activities beyond their boundaries, to respond to the challenges and opportunities presented by a world characterized by an increasing need for innovation and by the structural presence of digital networks (Section 1.4).

1.2   THE ORGANIZATION OF INNOVATION

Innovative activity is fraught with risk. Innovation risk tends to be higher for radical innovations and lower for incremental ones. The risk also varies with the industry. For instance, the risk might be greater in the physical/ tangible goods sector than in the services sector, because services can be experimented more easily than products. The risk might also be greater in business-to-consumer markets than in business-to-business markets, due to the large number of customers in the former and the difficulty of directly understanding customer needs.

In Figure 1.1, we illustrate the relationship between the fixed costs, the variable costs, and the revenues from the new product over time. The return on investment is unpredictable both in terms of its magnitude as well as in the timing of the payoff. Three points in time are particularly important on the cost/payoff curve.

The first point (T0) marks the beginning of the firm's investment in the innovation. This investment increases and plateaus at the end of the innovation project. The second point (T1) refers to the market launch of the innovation. At this point, the new product starts producing revenues. The third point (T2) indicates the point when the revenues exceed the initial investment, which includes the fixed costs in planning the innovation, as well as the fixed and variable costs of managing the production and launch of the new product. This last point is a crucial milestone, as it determines when the innovation starts generating positive economic flows and contributes to the firm's profitability. Of course, the majority of new products

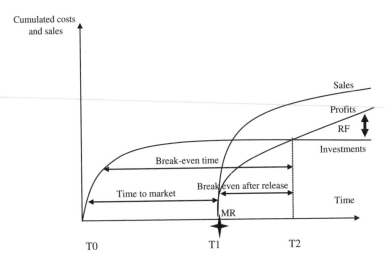

Source: House and Price (1991).

Figure 1.1 Financial evolution of product innovation: the 'return map'

never reach the point of launch or achieve breakeven (Urban and Hauser, 1993).

How should firms organize themselves to reduce the risks of innovation? One approach is to break down the process into a number of defined stages to ensure that failures are caught early and cheaply (for example, Urban and Hauser, 1993; Ulrich and Eppinger, 1999; Crawford and Di Benedetto, 2006). The key stages in the process are:

- *Creating the ideas* Idea generation is based on managerial intuition as well as on the analysis of the resources of the firm, the degree of technological maturity, the characteristics of the industry, the competitive offerings, macroenvironmental factors (laws, policies, social customs and so forth), and outcomes of R&D and market research.
- *Selecting the ideas* The ideas generated are culled based on the customer acceptance, the cost, the technological feasibility and the development cost.
- *Developing the prototype* This stage involves the creation of product/service prototypes to test the product's technical and economic feasibility, and evaluate the customer reaction to the product.
- *Developing the product* This stage involves the development of the final product and the validation of demand and product performance through product or market tests.

Table 1.1   *Financial investments at different stages of the innovation process*

Stage	1968	1982	1995
Creating the ideas	5%	10%	10%
Selecting the ideas	5%	10%	15%
Developing the prototype	15%	20%	20%
Developing the product	15%	15%	18%
Launch	60%	45%	37%

Source: Castaldo et al. (1995).

- *The launch*   This last step entails final product testing, the commercialization of the product and monitoring of the product's performance in the market after it has been launched.

The investments that firms make in the innovation process vary dramatically by stage in the process (Booz, Allen & Hamilton, 1968, 1982). A study of a representative sample of the complex and diversified US industrial industry showed that in the late 1960s, the technical and production stages and commercial launch of the product usually absorbed most of the investments. However, this emphasis on the later stages meant a higher risk of failure, as mistakes tend to be propagated too far into the process before they are detected. In this study, the prevailing high failure rate of new products was attributed to the fact that the real potential of the product was not carefully considered due to the inadequate financial investments made in the initial phases of the process. The study estimated that half of the overall resources invested in product innovation were for products withdrawn from the market (Table 1.1). A later study carried out by Booz, Allen & Hamilton found an increase in the investments that firms made in the early stages of the process relative to the investments they made in the later stages. This emphasis on front-end investments resulted in a 29 per cent decrease in the resources invested in new products withdrawn from the market. A more recent study carried out in Europe confirmed this general trend (Castaldo et al., 1995). These results suggest that firms need to focus more on the early stages of product innovation, because these investments have a highly leveraged downstream effect. They also suggest that firms need to find flexible venues in order to adapt to markets characterized by changing needs, wants, preferences, and therefore high risks.

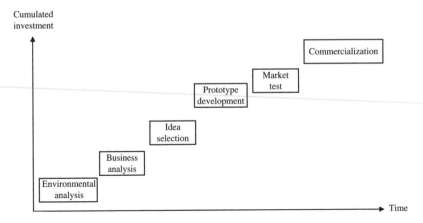

Cumulated investment

Commercialization

Market test

Prototype development

Idea selection

Business analysis

Environmental analysis

Time

Source: Sommers (1982).

Figure 1.2 The 'rational approach' to new product development

1.3 STRATEGIC ORIENTATION AND COMPETITIVE ADVANTAGE IN THE PROCESS OF INNOVATION

How do firms organize in order to minimize the risks of the new product development process? The rationalistic approach, which relies on making decisions based on rationality, is a popular reference point when dealing with the development of innovations and organizing for innovation. The origins of the rationalistic approach date back to the methods adopted by large firms to create new products between the 1950s and 1960s. A seminal development in this connection was the phased project planning (PPP) developed by NASA in the early 1960s for the Apollo moon exploration mission (Cooper, 1988; Spencer, 1990). In the rationalistic approach, the innovation process is divided into a number of phases, with each phase representing a set of activities needed to transform an innovative idea into a finished product. The innovation process is a highly structured set of stages. Each stage is followed by a 'gate' – a decision point for allowing the innovation project to move forward or to be abandoned (Cooper, 1988). In Figure 1.2, we show a typical representation of this rational and structured approach to product innovation.

In the rationalistic approach, the development of the innovation is considered to be a process that must be carried out sequentially. Each stage requires specialized competences and produces an innovative semifinished product – an idea, a prototype, a product – that is an input to the subsequent stage. The sequential approach can be traced back to a division of innovation work along functional lines, and to a method of interaction between the functions that is sequential – marketing followed by design followed by engineering and so on (Sommers, 1982). The sequential interaction forces each functional area to be involved in the innovative process, and it assumes that the work of each functional area can be performed independently, and can wait until the work of the function that managed the previous stage is completed. This is a fairly rigid approach, and the classic 'stage-gate' process does not permit significant adaptation or flexibility.

With the increase in environmental complexity and the rise of hyper-competition, adaptation is a key requirement. Therefore, several scholars in the innovation literature have suggested a different approach to managing innovation (for example, Leonard-Barton, 1995; Nonaka and Takeuchi, 1995; Tushman and O'Really, 1997; Govindarajan and Trimble, 2006). More recently, scholars studying managerial cognition have also argued for a different approach (for example, Gavetti and Levinthal, 2000), called the 'cognitive approach'. The cognitive approach is motivated by the realization that the process of innovation relies heavily on the process of knowledge creation and use.

A good example of the cognitive approach to innovation is the approach followed by the clothing distribution sector in Belgium (Danneels, 2003). The model of market activation, represented in Figure 1.3, features a learning process where the activities undertaken go hand in hand with the

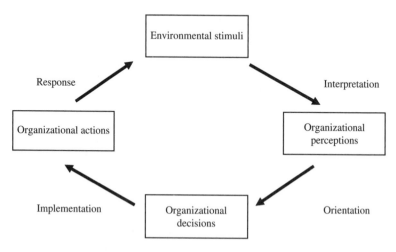

Source: Danneels (2003).

Figure 1.3   The process of market enactment in the 'cognitive approach'

interpretation of the events and environmental signals, and this interpretation in turn guides the firm's strategic choices. In the cognitive approach, traditional planning gives way to in-field learning and learning by doing, allowing firms to adapt better to complex and dynamic contexts.

The importance of the learning processes in the cognitive approach demands an organizational configuration that enables a rich interchange of individual actors involved in product innovation (Nonaka and Takeuchi, 1995). These learning processes are designed to:

- proactively shape the external environment, rather than react to the environment; and
- produce and rapidly disseminate the knowledge needed to create new products.

With regard to the firm's orientation towards its environment, a complex and dynamic environment makes it difficult for firms to adapt the innovation process to environmental needs/requirements. So the cognitive approach suggests that firms need to take a proactive approach by continuously 'probing and learning' – continual experimentation to generate new knowledge. Moving away from the logic of adaptation does not imply eliminating the role of the environment in the innovation process; what changes is the role that it plays. Instead of the environment being a source of information to which the organization adapts in a passive manner, the cognitive approach to product innovation envisages a continuous interaction between company knowledge and the knowledge of the numerous actors in the outside environment – customers, suppliers, researchers, universities and so forth (Powell et al., 1996).

With regard to the production and dissemination of knowledge, the knowledge produced during the learning process is stored in specific routines (Nelson and Winter, 1982; Teece et al., 1997) that, in order to be effectively used during the process, have to be integrated and used with the knowledge that the firm already possesses. Therefore, it is important to create an innovation process that allows different actors to work together in parallel to develop the new product. This parallel approach to product innovation has been discussed extensively in the product innovation literature both in the USA (Quinn, 1985; Clark and Fujimoto, 1991; Iansiti, 1997; Chesbrough, 2005) and Japan (Imai et al., 1985; Nonaka and Takeuchi, 1995). Due to the parallel execution of some of the typical stages of the innovation process and the parallel use of different competences, this structure can reduce product development time (greater efficiency) and also stimulate the creativity of those involved in the process (greater effectiveness). In fact, the possibility of developing numerous parallel solutions increases the number of available options the company has (Iansiti, 1997; Cusumano, 1997).

1.4 ENHANCING PRODUCT INNOVATION THROUGH DISTRIBUTED COMPETENCES

Despite the increasing relevance of the cognitive over the rational approach, it is interesting to note that firms have today been faced by a second challenge: the increasing need for change (Table 1.2). Continuous innovation in fact becomes a key strategy in the new competitive landscape. And in order to pursue innovation on a systematic basis, companies are being forced to rethink the boundaries by which they generate ideas and bring products to market. Increasingly, they are leveraging external ideas together with their in-house R&D competences. While most executives agree that continuous innovation is a competitive necessity, they would also agree that their innovation processes are not yielding the desired results. So firms need to look beyond their boundaries for help with innovation. According to a study conducted by Linder et al. (2003) in five industries – pharmaceuticals, high technology/electronics, automotive, retail, and oil and chemicals – the share of innovative ideas coming from external sources was estimated to be an average of 45 per cent of the total ideas, with this figure being as high as 90 per cent for some retail companies.

Faced with this reality of reduced innovation productivity, firms are moving beyond a closed model of innovation, which emphasizes control and self-reliance in R&D. As suggested by Chesbrough (2003 and 2006), they are instead starting to embrace an open innovation approach. The boundary between the individual company and its surroundings is becoming porous. Rather than all the innovative competences residing inside the firm, the innovation value chain is becoming more dispersed. External R&D has the benefit of providing valuable ideas without significantly increasing the fixed costs for R&D, while internal R&D remains necessary to develop the ideas and make them market-ready. The firm does not have to originate the research in order to profit from its results (Chesbrough, 2003).

The diffusion of information and communication technologies (ICTs) even makes openness a more viable alternative to sustain innovation. The explosion of connectivity, along with the development of new information standards, permits an open and almost cost-free exchange of information between actors in any market (for example, Shapiro and Varian, 1998; Evans and Wurster, 1999). One of the consequences of this phenomenon is that knowledge is progressively becoming more distributed and more

Table 1.2 Continuous innovation in the new competitive landscape

Firm	Industry	Best-practice re-innovation
Intel	ICT (microprocessors)	Double the transistor capacity every 18 months
		Build a new product plant every 9 months
3M	Adhesives	Produce every year 30% of the sales with new products (launched in the last 3 years)
British Airways	Airlines	Redefine every 5 years the core characteristics of the airline service on board and in the airport
Starbucks	Fast food	Launch 300 new points of sale every year up until 2000
		Develop new product concept every 6 months
Ducati	Motorbikes	Contact the current customers to redefine accessories every year
		Development of Ducati Monster for Tech café
Microsoft	ICT (software and operating systems)	Upgrade operating system every 3 years
Apple	ICT (hardware and software)	'Think differently': launch really new products in related industries
		Redesign new products every two years
Amazon.com	e-Commerce	Redefinition of the assortment depth every 3 months
		Redefinition of the assortment width every 3 months
Oticon	Hearing aids	Developing a product every 2 years
		Leading the characteristics of innovation within the industry

Source: Adapted from Brown and Eisenhardt (1998).

specialized. Digital networks allow a large number of players to systematically share ideas and create distributed learning systems (Sproull and Kiesler, 1991). Hence, knowledge is becoming more diverse as industries converge and markets collide (Prahalad and Ramaswamy, 2004). Firms need to cast their nets far and wide to garner the knowledge they need to create new products and processes (Powell et al., 1996).

As a consequence, geography is becoming less important in defining the boundaries of a firm's scope from both the organizational and technical viewpoints. Not only do markets become more global and demand an enlargement of the organizational domain, but the value chain that firms use to manage the strategic and operation activities is becoming more dispersed to capture these emerging opportunities. In a networked world, firms can shrink or expand their scope of operations whenever it is efficient to do so (Afuah, 2003).

The distribution of competences and activities across organizations and geographies has important implications for managing the innovation process. The ability of firms to divide innovative labor beyond their boundaries has historically been limited by several factors, including the absence of open standards and the idiosyncrasy of knowledge (Arora and Gambardella, 1994). For these reasons, an interorganizational division of innovation has historically been limited to a few industries such as biotechnology (for example, Shan et al., 1994; Powell et al., 1996), pharmaceuticals (for example, Cockburn et al., 2000), and the automotive industry (for example, Langlois and Robertson, 1995; Dyer and Nobeoka, 2000). However, the Internet has become a ubiquitous medium, and has opened new doors for firms as they look for new ways of organizing innovative activity. ICTs make it possible to divide innovation-related activities among independent entities aligned by mutual self-interest, allowing a new model of distributed innovation to emerge.

Distributed innovation can be described as an innovation process with constitutive activities dispersed in space, connected in diverse and asynchronous ways and involving heterogeneous actors (Rammert, 2002). It aims at leveraging the 'wisdom of the periphery' and as a consequence, it requires interorganizational mechanisms to coordinate fragmented and parallel activities of innovation, which can be developed even outside the core organization (Coombs and Metcalfe, 2000). The key idea underlying this model is that innovation-related tasks can be partitioned into smaller activities that can be addressed more effectively by independent specialized actors, who can be either individuals or organizations, according to the contingent knowledge needs.

Several key phenomena are contributing to the push towards distributed innovation. The increased specialization of knowledge domains, combined with the enhanced dispersion of knowledge sources across different actors and geographies, make the distribution of innovation activities essential in order to leverage the best-available competences. When knowledge for innovation is broadly distributed, the locus of innovation tends to shift from the firm to a network of interorganizational relationships (Powell et al., 1996). Further, markets are becoming more fragmented. In fragmented markets, knowledge tends to be distributed more widely among different actors and to become embedded in the shared infrastructure connecting such actors. Therefore, there is a need for a reaggregation of the actors (Sawhney and Parikh, 2001). In addition to the fragmentation of markets, knowledge is becoming more modular (Baldwin and Clark, 1991). Strategies based on modularity have emerged as a good way to deal with the quickening pace of change. Modularity is based on the ability to build a complex product or process from smaller subsystems that can be designed independently yet function together as a whole (Baldwin and Clark, 1997). Modularity facilitates the retention and reuse of system parts and enhances the speed, scope and reach of innovation (Garud et al., 2002). When applied to knowledge creation, modularity can be gained by decomposing the knowledge required in the innovation process into modules that can be independently produced and later combined. Consequently, in a distributed innovation system, some actors can focus on the production of knowledge modules and benefit from economies of scale, while others can focus on combining and adapting these modules of knowledge into whole solutions.

Another consequence of the rapid pace of change and uncertainty in dynamic markets is that firms can become trapped within their immediate field of view, and suffer from core rigidities that result from self-referential learning (Leonard-Barton, 1995). Dynamic market settings require firms to continually reconfigure their organizational architecture so that they can generate double-loop learning (Argyris and Schön, 1978). In these settings, firms need to continuously absorb knowledge and transform such knowledge into new products (Teece et al., 1997). Moreover, in such contexts, firms face the speed limit problem in absorption (Zahra and George, 2002). Learning cycles cannot easily be shortened and some of the resources needed to absorb innovative knowledge directly from the market may not be combined quickly within the organization (Clark and Fujimoto, 1991). This is also true in nascent markets where customer needs are poorly understood and evolve rapidly. In such contexts, firms need to sequence new products rapidly (Helfat and Raubitschek, 2000) and continuously introduce innovations (Eisenhardt and Martin, 2000). To support this pace of innovation, firms need to tap into additional sources of knowledge and set up ad hoc innovation-sourcing channels to meet particular business needs (Linder et al., 2003). This dynamic pattern is especially true in the case of converging industries. When industries tend to converge and industry boundaries tend to blur rapidly, unrelated skills from different worlds also tend to converge (Andal-Ancion et al., 2003). In those cases, it is much less likely that a single firm will possess all the competences needed for innovation. Leveraging distributed innovation becomes the best solution to fill the gap.

Specifically, as Weber (2004) suggests, four organizational principles are important in enabling distributed innovation: empower people to experiment; enable bits of information to find each other; structure information so that it can recombine with other pieces of information; and, finally, create a governance system that sustains this process. Leading companies such as Procter & Gamble and Nokia have developed a separate organizational unit responsible for establishing and managing new external sources for innovation. They evaluate relationships regularly and measure the competitive effectiveness of each external channel for augmenting internal innovation (Linder et al., 2003).

To make distributed innovation work, several conditions need to be satisfied (Sawhney and Prandelli, 2000). Disaggregated contributions need to be derived from knowledge that is accessible under clear, non-discriminatory conditions, without being proprietary or locked up. The product has to be perceived as important and valuable for a critical mass of users, and it has to benefit from widespread peer attention and review, potentially being improved through creative challenge and error correction. Usually, pure distributed innovation systems are characterized by an individual or a small group that can take the lead and generate a substantive core that promises to evolve into something truly useful. In the best cases, a voluntary community of iterated interaction can develop around the process of building the product. Notwithstanding the characteristics of the product and the nature of the contributor, a committed sponsor is always needed to coordinate the distributed innovation process, as well as proper incentives and mechanisms for sharing payoffs in order to motivate all the participants to put their individual competences at the service of the entire system.

In the next chapter, we highlight how a firm can play the role of a sponsor in promoting and orchestrating distributed innovation, and how it can harness the creative contributions of its customers in a networked digital environment in order to generate collaborative innovation.

NOTE

1. As we highlighted in the Introduction, we define 'distributed innovation' as the phenomenon of extending innovation beyond a firm's boundaries; we define 'collaborative innovation' as the specific co-creation activities that more particularly concern the customer–firm relationship.

2. The promise of collaborative innovation

2.1 INTRODUCTION

In an increasingly dynamic business environment, firms are realizing the importance of collaboration for creating and sustaining competitive advantage. Collaboration with partners and even competitors has become a strategic imperative for firms in the networked world of business (Brandenburger and Nalebuff, 1996; Gulati et al., 2000; Iansiti and Levien, 2004). In recent years, scholars in strategy and marketing have paid considerable attention to collaboration with customers to co-create value (Thomke and von Hippel, 2002; Prahalad and Ramaswamy, 2004). Nurturing relationships with customers is a priority for most organizations (for example, Day, 2000) at a time when customer intimacy, customer equity and customer relationship management are considered the current marketing mantras (Bhattacharya and Sen, 2003) and relationship marketing is seen as the key to building customer loyalty (for example, Garbarino and Johnson, 1999). While collaboration with customers can span several business processes, one of the most important is collaborating to co-create new offerings.

In this chapter, we propose that virtual environments play a key role in enhancing co-creation with customers by presenting low-cost opportunities for customers to interact with firms. The unique capabilities of the Internet are allowing leading firms to directly involve customers in their new product development (NPD) activities, a phenomenon we call 'collaborative innovation'. Customer interaction has always been important in NPD in order to improve the fit between the firm's offerings and customer needs (von Hippel, 1988). In Section 2.2, we provide an overview of the academic literature related to customer knowledge and customer involvement in marketing and innovation. In Section 2.3, we highlight how firms can create virtual customer environments to tap into customer knowledge through an ongoing dialogue (Sawhney and Prandelli, 2000a; Nambisan, 2002). The Internet enhances the ability of firms to engage customers in collaborative innovation in several ways. It allows firms to transform episodic and one-way customer interactions into a persistent dialogue with customers. Through the creation of virtual customer communities, it allows firms to tap into the social dimension of customer knowledge shared among groups of customers with shared interests. It also extends the reach and the scope of the firm's customer interactions through the use of independent third parties to reach non-customers – competitors' customers or prospective customers.

Section 2.4 shows how recent developments in Internet technologies, such as multimedia and Web 2.0 technologies further enhance the capabilities that firms can leverage to engage with customers. Finally, in Section 2.5, we formally introduce the notion of collaborative innovation to set the agenda for the remainder of the book.

2.2   CUSTOMER KNOWLEDGE: AN OVERVIEW

Collaboration has become an established way of doing business with suppliers, channel partners and complementors. However, except for a few notable exceptions, working directly with customers to co-create value remains a somewhat foreign notion for firms. As consumers have become increasingly empowered and demanding, marketing scholars have preached the benefits of customer-relationship management – essentially an 'inside-out' approach to retaining customers based on the misguided notion that the company is the arbiter of the relationship and the customer plays a passive role. This inside-out approach greatly underplays the potential role that direct customer involvement can play in value creation (for example, Firat and Venkatesh, 1995; Wikström, 1996; Gummeson, 1998).

Customer participation in innovation *per se* is not a new concept. What is new is the recognition that encouraging customers to be 'co-producers' is the emerging frontier in competitive effectiveness (Bendapudi and Leone, 2003). As customers have begun to expect customized consumption experiences (Firat et al., 1995), they are more willing to co-create unique value for themselves (Prahalad and Ramaswamy, 2003). As such, firms can leverage the expertise and creativity of their customers to increase the productivity of innovation (Lovelock and Young, 1979). Firat and Venkatesh (1995) argue that customers are demanding a specific role in production, and to satisfy them, marketers are required to open up more and more of their processes and systems to consumers' active participation. This active participation is a well-established approach in the service industry (for example, Schneider and Bowen, 1995; Lengnick-Hall, 1996). The ways in which the firm benefits from customer participation have been quantified in terms of productivity gains, with customer labor substituting for employee labor (for example, Lovelock and Young, 1979; Mills et al., 1983;

Mills and Morris, 1986). More generally, it has been pointed out that customer participation in value creation may have important effects on customer satisfaction (for example, Czepiel, 1990; Wind and Rangaswamy, 2001). It also enhances the firm's potential for innovation (Urban and von Hippel, 1988) and can increase the likelihood of new product success and product-market fit (Brown and Eisenhardt, 1995; von Hippel, 2001b).

The relationship between a firm and its customers in the co-creation of new products can evolve through several levels, from simple one-way communication to sophisticated interaction and dialogue. At the simplest level of the firm–customer interaction, customers play the role of passive receivers of the firm's innovation activities. The key idea at this stage is to improve the fit between the firm's offerings and customer needs by surveying customers and importing customer understanding into the firm (von Hippel, 1977). Firms need to listen to their customers by developing market orientation (Kohli and Jaworski, 1990), because market knowledge plays a strategic role in supporting their competitive advantage (Day and Wensley, 1988) by improving NPD processes (Donath, 1992; Dougherty, 1992). Market-sensing ability (Day, 1994) and internal organization are key factors driving innovation success (Verona, 1999), along with effective R&D and manufacturing routines (Hayes et al., 1988). Firms try to understand the expressed desires of their customers, called the 'voice of the customer' (Hauser and Clausing, 1988), usually through focus groups, customer surveys and research techniques such as concept testing and conjoint analysis (Leonard-Barton and Rayport, 1997). 'Listen carefully to what your customers want and then respond with new products that meet or exceed their needs' seems to be the mantra that has dominated many businesses in the recent past (Thomke and von Hippel, 2002). At this level, the firm–customer relationship tends to be a one-way import of explicit knowledge from individual customers that are already part of the company's customer base.

However, customer knowledge can play a much broader role in the firm's innovation processes and customer participation in innovation can be extended across three important dimensions (see Figure 2.1).

From Explicit Customer Knowledge to Tacit Customer Knowledge

When customers are viewed as passive recipients of the company's value proposition, the firm cannot fully understand customer knowledge assets developed within their specific contexts of experience. At the next level, firms can involve customers more deeply in their marketing process by developing two-way learning relationships with individual customers. Research in the service marketing field proves that customers can play the

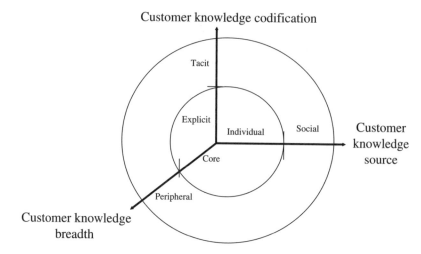

*Figure 2.1   Three expanding dimensions for customer knowledge
              absorption*

role of partial employees (Bowen, 1986; Mills and Morris, 1986). Such two-
way learning relationships enable the firm to create customized offerings for
specific target segments, greatly increasing their satisfaction (Leonard-
Barton, 1995). To support this two-way process, the firm's research toolkit
has to expand dramatically, as traditional market research only manages to
skim the surface of user needs and desires (Tidd et al., 2001). Firms need
to augment their repertoire of research tools with techniques aimed at discovering unarticulated needs through direct customer observation and
interaction. Firms can observe customers within their native surroundings
(Leonard-Barton and Rayport, 1997); enter dialogue and work closely
with lead users (von Hippel, 1986; Tabrizi and Walleigh, 1997); conduct
market experiments by using a 'probe and learn' process (Hamel and
Prahalad, 1994; Lynn et al., 1996); and adopt techniques designed to
uncover unarticulated, perhaps even unconscious preferences by surfacing
the metaphors, constructs and mental models driving customer thinking
and behavior (Zaltman and Higie, 1993; Zaltman, 1997).

Going even further, firms can involve customers directly in their product
design process. Techniques based on participatory design (Anderson and
Crocca, 1993; Carmel et al., 1993) and emphatic design (Leonard-Barton
and Rayport, 1997) enable customers to directly contribute to NPD. In
summary, one-way knowledge import evolves into a richer dialogue with
individual customers, allowing firms to tap into the deep and rich store of
tacit customer knowledge.

From Individual Customer Knowledge to Social Customer Knowledge

When firms interact with individual customers in innovation, an important dimension of customer knowledge still remains untapped. This is the social knowledge that develops through the interactions that customers have with each other (Martin and Clark, 1996) in order to develop a social identity and recognize themselves as members of specific social categories (for example, Kramer, 1991). Such knowledge creation tends to be deeply rooted in the social relationships that develop among various actors, and it has to be viewed from the sociological perspective on knowledge and value creation (for example, Spender, 1996; Nahapiet and Ghoshal, 1998; Nonaka and Konno, 1998). According to the sociological approach, relationships between several kinds of knowledge are social relationships between the individuals and the groups who develop and possess them (Böhme, 1997). Consequently, creating new knowledge means creating new relationships or new ways to combine and manage existing relationships (Troilo, 2001). The sociological perspective views knowledge creation as an emerging, dynamic and diffuse process (Youngblood, 1997). New knowledge is the output of a synergistic interplay between individual contributions and social interactions. These interactions foster the development of a common meaning that transcends individual contributions, like in the *ba* of Nonaka and Konno (1998), where knowledge creation is achieved by self-transcendence, through a spiralling process of interactions between explicit and tacit knowledge, involving individuals as well as organizations. Social knowledge is a crucial dimension of customer knowledge for supporting innovation, particularly in industries characterized by rapid and uncertain changes in customer preferences.

In recent years, researchers have become more aware of the relevance of social knowledge (for example, Peterson, 1995; Iacobucci and Ostrom, 1996). Some authors have introduced notions such as 'communitas' (Arnould and Price, 1993), 'communality' (Goodwin, 1994), or 'community' (Wenger, 1998) in order to describe the social and emotional phenomena in consumption. These authors suggest that customers choose specific products based not only on their usage value, but also on their linkage value, that is, their potential for stating customer identification with a specific social group (Godbout and Caillé, 1992). Hence, any consumption experience needs to be analyzed within a social context in order to be deeply understood (Douglas and Isherwood, 1979). The techniques that have been most commonly employed to analyze the influence of the social dimension on consumption behavior range from the traditional workshop based on focus groups, where the main challenge is dealing with groupthink phenomena, to anthropology (for example, McCracken, 1990; Sherry,

1995) and ethnography (for example, Jessor et al., 1996; Denzin, 1997), with its emphasis on cool hunting (Leonard and Swap, 1999). Especially in the last case, the main idea is that 'people within a culture have procedures for making sense' (Feldman, 1995: 8). Hence, the key object of the analysis is the bundle of verbal and behavioral mechanisms through which a specific group of customers build up social meaning. Participant observation, that is, observation of customer activities directly sharing their experiences on real time, is the most popular method for this purpose (Jorgensen, 1989). Techniques based on role playing have been effectively used as well in order to grasp tacit knowledge at a collective level.

From Core Customer Knowledge to Peripheral Customer Knowledge

Firms can also benefit from intermediaries or 'knowledge brokers' that collect customer-generated knowledge from a broader set of contexts and from different vantage points (Hargadon, 1998; Hargadon and Sutton, 2000). Through direct channels of communication, companies may not be able to reach the right customers, because their interactions and perspectives tend to be limited to the markets they already serve, with all the risks of myopia that Christensen and Bower (1998) point out. Companies can also find it difficult to reach people at the right time, because customers tend to interact with them at relatively late stages of the decision-making process. Knowledge brokers can connect with a broader base of customers than the firm's own customers, in contexts that are very different from the narrow context of product purchasing, and in domains that extend beyond the firm's immediate product and service offerings. Therefore, they help individual firms to listen to more diverse and unusual voices, accessing customer knowledge that is not only individual and social, explicit and tacit, but also not constrained by the firm's mental models or biases. By improving the 'peripheral vision' of firms, these mediators help firms to escape from the tyranny of their served markets and their core customer knowledge (Hamel and Prahalad, 1994).

2.3   THE ROLE OF THE WEB IN SUPPORTING COLLABORATION WITH CUSTOMERS

Despite the broad rhetoric on customer involvement in the firm's innovation activities, customers still play a limited and largely passive role in the development of new products in most industries (Wayland and Cole, 1997). While there are several reasons for this practice, a key limiting factor is the poor connectivity between customers and producers, especially in business-to-consumer markets. Cooperation with customers has always been the rule in business-to-business markets where there are just a few large and competent clients, who often require made-to-order production. However, business-to-consumer markets tend to have large and widely dispersed customer bases, so it is not feasible to create a dialogue with millions of individual consumers.

The Internet offers several new capabilities that not only make customer knowledge absorption easier and cheaper, but also allow customers to engage actively in the firm's innovation activities. Specifically, web-based tools can simplify the activities of customer knowledge absorption by making it easier and cheaper to manage systematic interactions with selected customers and even prospective customers. The Internet enables the creation of virtual customer environments – platforms for collaboration that allow firms to tap into customer knowledge through an ongoing dialogue (Sawhney and Prandelli, 2000a; Nambisan, 2002). The market can be conceived as a forum in digital settings, and value can be co-created at multiple points of interaction through systematic cooperation between companies and well-informed, networked, empowered and active customers (Prahalad and Ramaswamy, 2004). Co-opting customer competence becomes feasible thanks to the Internet; in virtual environments, companies have to recognize that the dialogue with their customers is a dialogue of equals (Prahalad and Ramaswamy, 2000). Consider the well-known example of open-source software development. This community-based innovation approach is shifting the locus of innovation to communities of users, and greatly increasing the scale and reach of creative communities. This community-based approach, where self-organized user groups collaborate online to create software applications, is proving to be a viable and low-cost alternative to proprietary software development using the traditional firm-centric approach to innovation (von Hippel, 2001a).

First, the Internet allows for a continuous and rich dialogue with a large number of customers at a very low cost (Evans and Wurster, 1999). Therefore, it makes the one-way customer knowledge import and dialogue with individual customers more efficient and effective. Second, the Internet vastly augments the firm's capacity to tap into the social dimension of customer knowledge by enabling the creation of virtual communities of consumption in order to collect and analyze knowledge that develops through spontaneous conversations among customers (Rheingold, 1993; Kozinets, 1999). Finally, the Internet presents new opportunities to access the competences and knowledge of partners' partners (Afuah, 2003), as well as the knowledge of customers' customers through electronic archives and virtual communities. Hence, firms can improve their 'peripheral vision' by

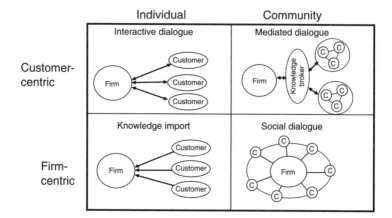

Figure 2.2   A taxonomy of collaboration mechanisms through virtual environments

grasping knowledge that lies beyond their immediate markets through independent third parties. By acting as knowledge brokers, they fill structural holes between individual customers and communities of customers on the one side and specific firms on the other. A description of the unique characteristics of the Internet that enhance customer involvement in the firm's innovation activities is contained in Figure 2.2.

Reach: Allowing Firms to Reach Beyond Current Customers, Markets and Geography

The Internet is an open, cost-effective and easy to use network relative to previous networks, such as electronic data interchange (EDI) that were proprietary and therefore costly to join or access (Afuah, 2003). These properties make the Internet a global medium with unprecedented reach, substantially increasing the number of relationships that every individual player can manage without any geographic constraints (Craincross, 1997). The Internet provides people with a vast amount of information, regardless of their location or time zone, lowering the search costs for finding exactly what they want or who they want. In this way, the Internet facilitates extended connectivity that is crucial for tapping into distributed competences (Andal-Ancion et al., 2003). It influences how organizations – and even customers – coordinate their activities, communicate, and collaborate to reduce costs and enhance the effectiveness of the firm's communications with customers and partners (Afuah and Tucci, 2000).

Interactivity: Permitting True Collaborative Work instead of Merely 'Knowledge Import'

Virtual environments break the age-old trade-off between richness and reach (Evans and Wurster, 1999). In this context, 'reach' simply means the number of people exchanging information. Richness is defined by three aspects of the information itself: the bandwidth, or the amount of information that can be moved from sender to receiver in a given time; the degree to which the information can be customized; and the level of interactivity. In the physical world, communicating (and absorbing) rich information requires physical proximity or dedicated channels, whose costs or physical constraints have limited the size of the audience to which the information could be sent. Conversely, the communication of information to a large audience has required compromises in bandwidth, customization and interactivity. In other words, sharing information with a large audience requires compromises in the quality of information. The number and the quality of relationships that any player can develop in the physical world are limited by this reach–richness trade-off. However, in virtual environments, it is possible to break this trade-off and create two-way relationships with a large number of players without compromising on the richness of the relationships. On the Web, companies can have rich interactions with a large set of customers on a systematic basis. The rapid emergence of universal technical standards for communication, which allow everybody to communicate with everybody else at essentially zero cost, is the fundamental driver of this new opportunity. In fact, the same technical standards underlie all the so-called 'Net' technologies: the Internet, which connects everyone; Extranets, which connect companies to one another; and Intranets, which connect individuals within companies. Those emerging open standards and the explosion in the number of people and organizations connected by networks are freeing information from the channels that have been required to exchange it, making those channels unnecessary or uneconomical and information a conveniently accessible asset (Evans and Wurster, 1997).

Scalability: Allowing Firms to Connect with Thousands of Customers

Positive network externalities create incentives to extend the number of connections enacted by an individual player. As Aghion and Tirole (1994: 350) indicates, 'positive network externalities arise when a good is more valuable to a user the more users adopt the same good or compatible ones'. On the supply side, the incremental cost to reach a new customer progressively decreases because of the predominance of fixed costs compared to variable costs (Shapiro and Varian, 1998). On the other side, consumers find more value in a network as the number of users increases (Gladwell, 2000; Cartwright, 2002). According to the so-called 'Metcalfe's law', the value of a network increases in proportion to the square of the number of people using it. The first competitor to achieve a critical mass of customers can potentially achieve dominance (Downes and Mui, 1998). As a consequence, when a company has reached the critical mass of connections, these connections tend to increase further in a virtuous cycle. However, the threshold level has a limit beyond which the value of the network may reduce because of the negative effects of a very large network – which include saturation, contamination and cacophony. Nonetheless, the threshold level of a virtual network is far greater than that of a physical network (McAfee and Oliveau, 2002). More generally, positive network externalities are particularly important to digital marketing and innovation because they may affect digital activities. Hence, common standards for digital communication, common formats for data exchange, and common platforms for computing can facilitate positive network externalities (Ruefli et al., 2001).

Persistence: Persistent Ongoing Engagement instead of Episodic Interactions

Advances in ICTs have made industries more global and have blurred the boundaries between industries (Prahalad and Ramaswamy, 2003). Therefore, the division of innovative labor can be made across geographies (Linder et al., 2003). The joint effect of geographical and industry convergence is that firms are much less likely to find all the competences needed to support innovation within their four walls. The Internet can be used to coordinate activities and information sharing between otherwise disconnected pools of knowledge and competences on a systematic and global basis, at a lower cost than in traditional, offline environments (Porter, 2001). It allows firms to outsource some activities that used to be performed internally – and vice versa – thereby either expanding or shrinking vertical firm boundaries (Afuah, 2003). Hence, virtual environments create the need for engaging an increasing number of players on a systematic basis (because of greater diversity in competences needed), and at the same time they provide the solution (low-cost coordination mechanisms and opportunities for sharing the innovative labor on a global and continuous basis). This phenomenon also creates a strong motivation for modularity as a strategy for designing products and product development processes efficiently; each module is designed independently but is designed to be part of a system that functions as an integrated whole. Modularity does more than accelerate the pace of change or heighten competitive pressure. It also transforms relations among companies. Being part of a shifting modular cluster comprising hundreds of companies in a constantly innovating industry is quite different from being one of a few dominant companies in a stable industry (Baldwin and Clark, 1997). Digital environments are accelerating this evolutionary path.

Speed: Reduced Latency in the 'Sense and Respond' Cycle

Real-time interfaces allow companies and customers to deal effectively with important information that changes suddenly and unpredictably (Andal-Ancion et al., 2003). The Internet has a powerful effect in increasing the flexibility of the firm's external network, allowing the firm to involve different partners at different times, and also allowing it to transform weak relations into strong relations and vice versa, depending on the complexity of the knowledge that needs to be transferred. Real time, two-way and low-cost communication makes it easy to consolidate specific customer relationships on a contingent basis through ad hoc virtual communities and online conversations (for example, Hoffman and Novak, 1996; Hagel and Singer, 1999). As a consequence, the individual players can benefit from high plasticity in their connections with different actors once a platform for interaction has been created (Prahalad and Krishnan, 2002).

Peer to Peer: Allowing Access to Customer-generated Social Knowledge

The Web also vastly augments the firm's capacity to tap into the social dimension of customer knowledge by enabling the creation of virtual communities of consumption to collect and analyze knowledge that develops through spontaneous conversations among customers. Customers self-select on the basis of the focused interests promoted by specific communities. This self-selection means that customers are highly involved and motivated to share knowledge with other customers and community managers, making their contribution both richer and less expensive than in the offline world. The phenomenon of 'word of mouth' epitomizes this concept. In the physical world, word of mouth is limited to conversations customers have with a few close peers or friends. In the virtual world, the picture is quite different. Virtual communities permit firms to systematically leverage social customer knowledge by harnessing the power of the so-called 'word-of-mouse' phenomenon (Reichheld and Schefter, 2000). Groupware, collaborative and messaging tools can also empower customers to help one another. This peer-based support can reduce the customer's need to rely on direct support from the company (Kambil et al., 1999).

Indirect Ties: Allowing Access to the Partners' Partners' Knowledge

While direct ties play a key role in determining the network access, *indirect ties* are also useful, because firms learn not only from the knowledge of their partners but also from the knowledge of their partners' partners (Gulati and Gargiulo, 1999; Ahuja, 2000). The Internet also serves as an important tool for generating indirect ties. As we said, it is a low-cost open platform (for example, Ruefli et al., 2001); anyone anywhere can connect to it and contribute to the public discussion. Therefore, it is easy to access the knowledge of partners once-removed from direct partners (Afuah, 2003), as well as the knowledge of customers' customers. The Internet positively impacts on the number of indirect ties that firms can develop because it allows them to access electronic archives and virtual communities of a partners' partner, absorb this already codified and digitalized knowledge, and recombine it in new ways.

Virtual environments also influence structural autonomy – the network property of having 'relationships free of structural holes at their own end and rich in structural holes at the other end' (Burt, 1992: 45). As we discussed earlier, firms are finding it increasingly difficult to gather all the competences needed to support innovation. As a result, emerging structural holes across industries need to be filled. The Internet can be used to coordinate activities and information sharing between otherwise disconnected pools of knowledge and competences on a global basis and at a lower cost than in traditional, offline environments (Porter, 2001; Afuah, 2003).

2.4   BEYOND THE FIRST-GENERATION INTERNET: TOWARDS THE INTEGRATED MULTIMEDIA NETWORK AND WEB 2.0 APPLICATIONS

The digitalization process has created new connections among industries that during the past were distinct and separate, such as telecommunication, consumer electronics, media, broadcasting and information technology. The opportunity to enter the Web is becoming more and more global and universal, no longer limited to specific access devices or media types. There are three major drivers of convergence (Doering and Parayre, 2000; Pagani, 2003). First, there is device convergence – among devices, such as personal digital assistants, mobile phones, digital television (digital cable, digital satellite and digital terrestrial), and notebooks with a wireless connection. Second, there is network convergence – among networks, such as modem and telephone, satellite and DSL. Third, there is network convergence – among content, such as information, music and the movies.

These phenomena, together with the development of new transmission systems – such as Broadband and the Universal Mobile Telecommunication Service – have given birth to a ubiquitous digital environment, which is interdependent and interoperable, characterized by multimedia features and interactivity. New tools are emerging that make the interaction among players more flexible and interpersonal (Kumar and Venkatesan, 2005). For instance, the combination of Web TV and information-sharing technologies even allows users that are not equipped with a personal computer to create a dialogue and enter online services which range from the World Wide Web to home shopping applications, from Digital Video Broadcasting to the Internet, from on-demand movies to video telephony (Pagani, 2003).

In a similar multichannel context, communication opportunities are changing for both the customer and the company (Rangaswamy and van Bruggen, 2005). The former is beginning to consider different points of interaction at different stages of the life cycle of his/her relationship with the company, expecting richer and richer experiences with companies that know him/her better and better. The latter can enhance the value created for the customer at each stage of the same relationship, making its customer relationship management activities more effective and thereby reducing the opportunities of customer switching to other competitors.

Specifically, user-driven online services, including MySpace, Wikipedia and YouTube, have broadened the original notion of the Web. They have expanded the Internet into an integrated multimedia network, relying on applications supporting user collaboration, such as peer-to-peer networking, blogs, podcasts and online social networks. This group of technologies is usually recognized as Web 2.0. The 2,847 worldwide respondents to a survey conducted by McKinsey in 2007 expressed their satisfaction with their Internet investments so far, recognizing that Web 2.0 technologies are strategic, and they plan to increase their investments in the future (Bughin and Manyika, 2007). Early adopters of these technologies are particularly satisfied and motivated to make further investments. Popular tools in terms of current and future usage include Web services, collective intelligence and peer-to-peer networking, that is, all applications especially relevant to support collaboration in innovation activities. 'Web services' are pieces of software that make it easier for different systems to communicate with one another automatically in order to pass information or conduct transactions. 'Collective intelligence' refers to any system that attempts to tap the expertise of a group rather than expecting an individual to make decisions. Technologies that contribute to collective intelligence include collaborative publishing and common databases for sharing knowledge. 'Peer-to-peer networking' can be defined as a technique for efficiently sharing files either over the Internet or within a closed set of users. It distributes files across many machines, often those of the users themselves; some systems retrieve files by gathering and assembling pieces of them from many machines. Social networking and blogs (short for Web logs) are also becoming increasingly diffused. The former refers to systems that allow members of a specific site to learn about other members' skills, talents, knowledge or preferences, in communities both within and outside the company. This is one method used to identify experts related to a specific field. 'Blogs' are online journals or diaries hosted on a website and often distributed to other sites or readers using Really Simple Syndication (RSS), so that people can subscribe to online distributors of blogs as well as news, podcasts (audio or video recordings), or other information.

All these technologies are being used to encourage collaboration inside the company or communicate with customers and business partners in a more systematic way. Within the context of new product development, this opens up a host of new collaborative innovation opportunities.

2.5   COLLABORATIVE INNOVATION: TOWARDS A CONCEPTUAL FRAMEWORK

In conclusion, it is widely acknowledged that firms have entered the emerging era of open innovation, where the boundaries between the firm and its surrounding environment are more porous (Chesbrough, 2003). We focus on the role in value creation of a specific actor in the firm's environment – its customers. We propose that the new capabilities of the Internet and the integrated multimedia network enable the firm to evolve from merely interacting with customers towards active collaboration with customers as partners in value creation. The differences between the former and the latter are quite relevant. In the first case, the interaction is the locus of economic value extraction as the firm and markets are considered as forums for value exchange. The main competitive issue for the individual firm relies on a better understanding of customers in order to create a superior value proposition *for* them. In contrast, when we move towards a perspective centered on firm–customer collaboration, the interaction becomes the locus of co-creation of value and value extraction and markets are forums for the co-creation of experiences (Prahalad and Ramaswamy, 2004). The main competitive issue for the firm is to create value propositions *with* its customers: the firm and its customer collaborate in co-creating value and then compete in extracting value.

Virtual environments offer two key enablers for collaborative innovation. First, the Internet *empowers* customers across all marketing and innovation activities. In virtual environments, customers have the opportunity to define what information they want and what products they are interested in. Therefore, they have increased control over the exchange process, pushing companies to change their information policies in dealing with them from opaqueness to transparency (Sawhney and Kotler, 2001). The balance of power between the company and the customer is shifting towards greater equality, and the boundaries between them are blurring (Berthon et al., 2000). Specifically, customers have the possibility to *self-inform*, as they can research products and issues on their own without relying on experts (such as in the medical websites WebMD.com and MedlinePlus.com). According to the 'Internet efficiency view', in digital environments where product information is separated from the physical product (Alba et al. 1997), customers are fully informed about processes and all available alternatives, reducing opportunities of profit for retailers (Bakos, 1997; Brynjolfsson and Smith, 2000). Hence, they can *self-compare* product features and prices against competing manufacturers with a few clicks of a mouse (for example, PriceGrabber.com and DealTime.com). Customers can also *self-police* by monitoring reputations of sellers to assure themselves of product and service quality (for example, eBay.com and BizRate.com). Finally, they can *self-organize*, creating or joining communities of interest or conducting conversations on products, interests, lifestyles or issues to share their experiences (for example, iVillage.com, Experts-Exchange.com), and *self-advise*, providing feedback for their peers on the basis of their experiences with products and manufacturers (for example, Amazon.com, PlanetFeedback.com, Epinions.com, Ciao.com).

Perhaps the most significant change in firm–customer relationships introduced by the Internet is the direct customer involvement in marketing, especially innovation activities, through ad hoc virtual interfaces. This is the second key enabler of collaborative innovation in digital environments. In fact, the Web allows firms to *involve* customers across all innovation activities, from new idea generation to product testing and launch on the final market. In 2005, for instance, 120 000 people around the world signed up to join Boeing's World Design Team, an Internet-based global forum that encourages participation and feedback while the company is developing its new airplane. Activities included message boards, conversations with the Boeing design team, and extensive discussions on what members liked and did not like about air travel today, as well as features they would like to see in their dream airplane. Recently, brands such as Coors Light and Mercedes Benz have invited customers to co-create advertising campaigns, while Fiat asked its customers to contribute to the definition of the design attributes of the new-born Fiat500 nine months before its launch on the market.

In virtual environments, customers can participate in a process of *collaborative generation* of value propositions, contributing their creativity and competences to the firm. They can then engage in *collaborative selection* of ideas and concepts that are more likely to be successful in the market. Next, they can take part in *collaborative design*, either by using ad hoc user toolkits for product design or co-designing the offering with the company or other customers. They can then play a key role in *collaborative development* of the same offerings. Users can contribute, both individually and through participation in virtual communities, to the final offering realization, leveraging their specific knowledge and skills. Finally, customers can help the company in *collaborative testing* and debugging its new products, as well as in launching new products in the market, taking part in viral marketing programs and originating word of mouth.

In the rest of the book, we examine in greater detail the specific interaction tools and organizational mechanisms that can enable collaborative innovation.

3. Tools for collaborative innovation

3.1 INTRODUCTION

As we have highlighted in the previous chapter, customers are proving to be an invaluable source of ideas and insights for product innovation in a wide range of categories, ranging from sportswear to mechanical equipment (von Hippel, 2001a). The application of customer knowledge enhances the innovation process and makes it possible for the firm to better satisfy market needs. However, absorbing customer knowledge is difficult from an organizational standpoint and costly from an economic one (Cohen and Levinthal, 1990; Zahra and George, 2002).

Recent contributions to the academic literature provide compelling evidence of how the Internet and, in general, information and communication technologies (ICTs) enhance a firm's capacity to absorb market knowledge and interact systematically with a broad set of consumers that even go beyond its customer base. In this chapter, we focus on the revolutionary potential of the Web to support product innovation. We begin in Section 3.2 with a discussion of different web-based mechanisms that can support each stage of the product innovation process. In particular, we review the literature on the tools enabled by the latest ICT developments to support new product development (NPD), following the seminal contribution by Dahan and Hauser (2002). Ideally, the value of customer involvement in innovation through the Web should be substantiated not only with theory (for example, Dahan and Hauser, 2002), but also with hard data. However, since this does not seem to be the case in the literature, there is a need for a study that empirically explores the extent to which companies are actually leveraging different forms of customer engagement in virtual customer environments at each stage of the innovation process. We present the results of such an exploratory study in Section 3.3. Specifically, we discuss the web-based mechanisms that support collaborative innovation in five industries – automobiles, motorcycles, consumer electronics, food and beverages, and toiletries. We conclude by suggesting an incremental approach for putting collaborative innovation into practice at any firm.

3.2 THE ROLE OF THE WEB AT EACH STAGE OF THE PRODUCT DEVELOPMENT PROCESS

The capacity of companies to absorb customer knowledge plays a key role across all the stages of the product development process. In recent years, several studies have demonstrated the central role of digital environments in absorbing customer knowledge (for example, Dahan and Hauser, 2002; Urban and Hauser, 2002). These studies emphasize the potential of the Web as a tool for adaptive co-development of new products. In this approach, consumers become co-developers of innovation with firms who systematically solicit customer feedback by using interactive prototyping techniques and adopting a rapid experimentation approach (Eisenhardt and Tabrizi, 1995; Iansiti and MacCormack, 1997; Tyre and von Hippel, 1997; Bhattacharya et al., 1998). Effectively designed websites can not only provide useful information to help consumers express their preferences, they can also contribute to increasing consumer trust, and consequently, customer willingness to share information (Urban et al., 2001). In particular, as summed up in Table 3.1, digital environments are extraordinarily powerful in supporting direct involvement of consumers throughout the innovation process. The cost of developing and testing virtual prototypes is much lower than physical prototypes, and virtual reality can significantly enhance the quality of the interaction with the consumers and the process of distributed learning (Dahan and Srinivasan, 2000). Hence, an approach based on the systematic, direct interaction with customers is becoming increasingly relevant in NPD. Building on a previous contribution (Prandelli et al., 2006b)[1]. In the subsequent discussion, we elaborate on the most significant web-based applications at each stage of the product innovation process.

Idea Generation

The early stage of NPD particularly benefits from the Web's potential to integrate and enhance consumer input. The simplest application is online questionnaires (Burke et al., 2001). In the search for successful new product ideas, the aim is to reduce uncertainty by identifying customers' preferences and interacting directly with them to absorb various potential stimuli which could open up new paths (Dahan and Hauser, 2002). Online surveys usually aim to improve selected aspects of the site, product or service, and financial incentives considerably increase the response rate. In order to enhance customer involvement through the Web during the idea generation stage, companies can also use suggestion boxes where users can express their own innovative ideas. A good example of this is the Ben & Jerry site, where users can contribute new ideas for both products (prepackaged ice-cream) and

Table 3.1 Web-based tools for innovation: a review of literature

Innovation process stage	Web-based tools	Literature review
Idea generation	'Contact the firm' option	Hagel and Armstrong (1997)
	Feedback session/survey	Thurow (1997)
	Suggestion box	Kozinets (1999)
	Complaints area	Sawhney and Prandelli (2000b)
	Virtual community	Burke et al. (2001)
	Formalized mechanisms of competition on new ideas	Urban and Hauser (2002)
	Agreement area to manage intellectual property rights	
	Customer advisor programs	
Idea selection	Analysis of other customers' opinions	Srinivasan et al. (1997)
	Virtual concept test	Montoya-Weiss et al. (1998)
	Focus group online	Weissman (1998)
		Dahan and Hauser (2002)
Product design	Product customization options	Lakhani and von Hippel (2000)
	Patents for new products	Lee and Cole (2000)
	Open-source mechanisms	Park et al. (2000)
	Design toolkits	Liechty et al. (2001)
	Virtual teams	MacCormack et al. (2001)
		von Hippel (2001a)
		von Hippel (2001b)
		Dahan and Hauser (2002)
		von Hippel and Katz (2002)
Product test	Virtual product test	Urban et al. (1996)
	Complete market test online	Thomke (1998)
		Thomke et al. (1998)
		Dahan and Srinivasan (2000)
Market launch	New product area	Armstrong and Hagel (1996)
	Events	Hagel and Rayport (1997)
	Customized newsletter	Peppers and Rogers (1997)
	Virtual communities	Jurvetson (2000)
	Virtual marketing	Kenny and Marshall (2000)
	Customized products selection	Reichheld and Schefter (2000)
	Mini websites	

Source: Prandelli et al. (2006b).

services (especially packaging and distribution) in a dedicated area of customer assistance and incentives are offered to reward the best ideas. Advanced applications of these dialogue windows are also found in the Procter & Gamble site (www.pg.com) for various product categories. In the 'Share Your Thoughts' section, customers can view past suggestions or advice given by other consumers regarding specific products and can express their degree of agreement, promoting a collective process for selecting new ideas.

When firms solicit ideas from customers, it is essential for them to establish clear rules regarding intellectual property rights (Thurow, 1997) and to create appropriate financial or social incentives for customers to share their creativity and expertise. Well-designed incentives can improve customer-based idea generation significantly (Toubia, 2004). For instance, motorcycle companies such as Ducati and Aprilia encourage direct customer participation by offering rewards such as spare parts for their motorcycles. Reward mechanisms can be introduced for the most competent customers to compete with each other in solving specific innovation problems. These mechanisms can include financial remuneration, which can be significant in some cases. For instance, the Innocentive.com site originally created by Eli Lilly provides reward mechanisms for the generation of new concepts in several industries, ranging from plastics to mass market consumer goods that can reach $1,000,000.

The Web also makes it easier for firms to handle complaints, and to use complaints as an input to improve their products and assuage dissatisfied customers. In advanced applications, customers can be provided with a range of specific e-mail addresses where they can send their complaints and ask for explanations. Accurate analysis of the complaints serves to stimulate and strengthen existing products, and can even lead to the introduction of innovative new products. Particularly useful is the technique of 'listening in' (Urban and Hauser, 2002) which involves recording and analyzing information exchanged between customers and experts who provide virtual advice in order to help them identify products that best satisfy their needs (Maes, 1999). The 'virtual consultant' tries to identify the respondent's ideal product while the designer can understand the product features that least satisfy customers, and subsequently question them in order to understand how to best address unmet needs (Urban, 2000).

New product and service generation can also benefit considerably from online virtual communities of customers, which bring together users with shared interests and who are willing to promote spontaneous online conversations to exchange opinions and experiences (Hagel and Armstrong, 1997; Kozinets, 1999). By encouraging direct and interactive communication in the online community, these groups generate knowledge regarding consumption shared at the social level, which is difficult to grasp using other research tools (Urban, 2000). Intangible incentives, such as social recognition and reputation (for example, exclusive access to a dedicated 'hall of fame'), are a good way to stimulate participation in communities emerging in consumer markets, while economic incentives are more common in business communities (Sawhney and Prandelli, 2000b). In these virtual communities, members often develop a high degree of involvement and affiliation, and the communities attract members with considerable enthusiasm and technical competence.

Idea Selection

Idea selection represents a critical stage in NPD because it balances creativity with economic viability. At this stage, the most important web-based tools include virtual concept testing and online focus groups. Virtual reality technology allows firms to develop different product concepts in great detail, so that consumers can compare individual product features and select the most convincing concepts. For instance, Volvo has created a site called www.Conceptlabvolvo.com, where users can express their preference for new automobile concepts proposed by the company, in terms of concept appeal and likelihood of market success. Users can also view the evaluations expressed by other consumers in real time. The fundamental reasoning behind such methods is similar to that of Srinivasan et al. (1997) who claim that if the cost of transforming the product concept into a prototype is low – as in virtual environments – it is opportune to move the selection stage as far up as possible in the innovation process. The earlier the prototype is designed and tested in the process, the greater the flexibility in making changes to the product design and features. This results in reduced product development time (Iansiti, 1995), better learning from low-cost mistakes (Thomke, 1998), and reduced risk of obsolescence of information collected at the beginning of the product development cycle (Eisenhardt and Tabrizi, 1995). A caveat to keep in mind for idea selection is that different customers might have different degrees of knowledge about a specific product, and virtual interfaces have to be flexible enough to accommodate these variations (Randall et al., 2004).

Another tool that is useful for web-based concept selection is the online focus group (Montoya-Weiss et al., 1998). This is the traditional research technique that relies on interaction with a group of customers, except that the focus group is conducted on the Web. Web-based focus groups can be much more efficient, and they do a better job in accessing difficult-to-reach segments of customers and prospects (Weissman, 1998). Online focus groups can be based on chat rooms or videoconference technology (Burke et al., 2001). New technologies such as Skype allow for very low-cost multipoint videoconferencing among globally distributed participants, without the need for expensive videoconferencing infrastructure.

In an online focus group, participants are identified according to their specific characteristics and asked to form virtual teams to discuss and evaluate different product concepts. A particularly important aspect of the online focus groups is the anonymity the Internet provides. Although the virtual setting results in less emotional involvement, it has the benefit that participants are less inhibited and less subject to the groupthink phenomenon, where the individual contributions merely reflect the views of the dominant member of the group (Nunamaker et al., 1997).

The so-called 'information pump' (Prelec, 2000) is based on virtual focus groups where participants are asked to express their opinions about new product concepts in order to identify the most successful ones. The aim is to make an objective evaluation of the quality and internal coherence of the participants' opinions, which are evaluated by an impartial expert as well as by other participants. In order to ensure that this method functions efficiently, information must be updated in real time and an appropriate system of incentives should be created for participants. This method is particularly useful as it makes it possible to objectively classify the opinions of individual participants regarding new product concepts, and it allows for the evaluation of the quality and reliability of each respondent (Dahan and Hauser, 2002).

Product Design

Once product concepts have been identified, they have to be organized in product configurations that can subsequently be tested on the market before they are launched. At this point, the key problem is to transform consumer priorities into design and engineering priorities by directly involving customers in identifying specific product features to be incorporated into the final product (Urban and Hauser, 1982 [1993]; Moore and Pessemier, 1993). Such a co-definition of the product's features in virtual environments can range from simply applying mass-customization tools to combine aesthetic and functional product features conceived in modular form, to developing cross-functional design teams which involve customers directly through the Web, to the complete product design by customers.

As suggested by Dahan and Hauser (2002), consumers can be asked to select different product attributes of new product concepts by applying web-based preference elicitation tools such as conjoint analysis. By using virtual interfaces which respondents enjoy navigating and which are relatively easy for the company to implement, it becomes possible to determine the main features that respondents prefer, the interactions among attributes, and the optimal attribute configuration. These techniques have been successfully applied to develop a wide range of products, from cameras and photocopiers to toys and detergents.

The most advanced applications of web-based conjoint analysis have led to the mass customization of products designed and sold through the Web (Randall et al., 2004), such as the Barbie dolls offered online by Mattel and the sneakers which can be purchased on the Nike site. Consumers seem to especially like the interface images which allow them to view the different product attributes and then combine them to create their ideal product configuration with a mere click of the mouse. This practice has found wide-spread acceptance in the automotive industry. The website created for the new Mini Cooper is a good example of such a practice. And in the Volvo and Fiat 'Build your Car' sections, as well as 'BMW Individual' or 'Audi Configurator', the companies allow users to combine colors, components, accessories and functional attributes of their automobile, and also put together financial and insurance services packages. General Motors has created a web-based tool (the GM Vehicle Advisor) that helps customers to choose the right automobile for them based on their preferences. This tool allows GM to collect quantitative data on customer preferences from hundreds of thousands of customers on an ongoing basis at very low cost. These data help product developers to understand how customer preferences are evolving with changing market conditions, and can guide the development and refinement of new concepts. As Park et al. show (2000), respondents can be asked to create their products by adding attributes to a basic model or by eliminating undesirable attributes from the most complete configuration.

Although most online tools for product design testing such as web-based conjoint analysis focus on absorbing knowledge 'about' the customer, more advanced tools can enhance the knowledge and competence 'of' the customer. For instance, by allowing customers to make modifications to existing products, or even to suggest ideas for entirely new products, digital environments allow customers to become co-designers and co-developers of new products (Thomke and von Hippel, 2002).

Toolkits for user innovation can be created using new technologies such as computer simulation to make NPD faster and less costly (von Hippel, 2001b). These toolkits first emerged in a primitive form in the 1980s in the high-tech field of custom integrated circuit design and manufacturing, where the cost of correcting any eventual error found late in the design or testing stages is prohibitively high (ibid.). Toolkits for user innovation are user-friendly tools for the configuration of new products that allow users to self-develop innovations. This eliminates the problem of sharing customer knowledge that is often 'sticky' and context specific, and therefore difficult to transfer (von Hippel, 1994). User toolkits overcome this problem by shifting need-related development tasks to the user. These toolkits usually support specific projects within a specific product category. Within this domain, the user is free to innovate, develop customized products through mechanisms of repeated trial and error, and even suggest new patents for the finished product. In this way, the user can create a preliminary design, simulate its development and prototyping, evaluate how the product will function when used, and proceed to systematically improve it until he/she is satisfied with the final version (von Hippel and Katz, 2002). User toolkits for innovation provide users with true design freedom, as opposed to merely choosing from lists of options provided by mass customization. For example, National Semiconductor offers an online toolkit called Webench (webench.national.com), an online design environment for circuit designers. Using tools from the Webench site, circuit designers can design and test new circuits, and can have prototype power supply kits delivered anywhere in the world in 48 hours.

Customer toolkits can be expanded to allow customers to customize products and even develop them through repeated trial and error. They can also be used to obtain customer suggestions on patents for finished products. Additionally, customer toolkits can be used by communities of customers to build upon designs that have been created by other customers, as in the case of designing new games for mobile phones (Piller et al., 2004). Prototyping and rapid experimentation are crucial in supporting this approach, which can systematically integrate the competence and experience of the consumer in the innovation process (Kalyanaram and Krishnan, 1997; Krishnan and Bhattacharya, 1998). A broad range of industries have begun to introduce these applications. For instance, in the software industry, it has been widely demonstrated that it is useful to promote consumer involvement in the co-definition of products by allowing users to download beta versions and asking them to identify possible bugs (MacCormack et al., 2001). Customer-driven, web-based toolkits to support innovation processes have also been successfully developed in computer circuits, plastics and consumer goods (Thomke and von Hippel, 2002).

User design mechanisms can also be used by virtual cross-functional teams created by companies that can include customers as well as company employees (Sawhney and Prandelli, 2000a). In this case, customers are treated as real partners in the innovation process, and they are encouraged to collaborate in specific projects. Customers undergo a careful selection process and they are offered appropriate incentives – often based on reward mechanisms and/or contests. Then, customers can participate in virtual design teams and collaborate with company employees from the marketing,

R&D and production functions. Networking systems and groupware technologies are used to support interaction and knowledge sharing within the organization (Shapiro, 1989; Carraca and Carrilho, 1996; Quinn et al., 1996; Day, 1998), as well as the integration of new with pre-existing knowledge (Anand et al., 1998; Hoopes and Postrel, 1999). The result is a systemic collaboration that goes far beyond knowledge transfer (Davenport and Prusak, 1998).

User design in virtual user communities relies on peer-based review and feedback, a central tenet of the open-source mechanism for development (Lee and Cole, 2000). As we shall analyze more deeply in the final chapter of this book, the open-source mechanism features communities that are completely run by and for the users and allow them to exchange opinions on specific technology-intensive products (Constant et al., 1996). In an open-source mechanism, each user does not necessarily develop the needed product or service alone – as in the individual application of the toolkits for user innovation. Rather, each member of the community benefits from innovative suggestions made by other users. In the case of software products, this means that each user can obtain a copy free of charge, legally study its source code, and modify and distribute it to others without any remuneration (Lakhani and von Hippel, 2000). Many studies show that these mechanisms are particularly useful in developing innovations in the software industry and for Internet start-ups (Iansiti and MacCormack, 1997). For instance, in its 'forum for technology developers' section, Nokia uses the open-source mechanism to develop new technologies applied to mobile phones and related services (VAS) and to connectivity applications for computers. Similarly, in its 'solution for partners and developers' area, HP has an HPOpenView program, where users have the opportunity to utilize different mechanisms in order to contribute to the R&D activities of the company's research team.

Open-source mechanisms have expanded into many different industries (for instance, sportswear) where systematic NPD is essential (von Hippel, 2001a). These distributed innovation mechanisms are successful because they enhance the reputation of each user who contributes to the final output and promote a reciprocal relationship in the creation of the final product. Moreover, the sense of responsibility towards the group and the awareness of the significant impact on the community are important motivators for qualified and knowledgable members (Kollock, 1999).

Product Testing

Digital environments can significantly contribute to simplifying and making the new product testing stage more efficient before launching a product on the market. New technologies such as rapid prototyping, simulation and combinatorial methods make it possible to generate and test different product versions (Thomke, 1998). Web-based tools further enhance this approach by exploiting the potential of virtual reality, three-dimensional images and animation to generate low-cost virtual prototypes that are fairly close to the quality and completeness of the physical one (Dahan and Srinivasan, 2000). On the Web, firms can simultaneously test different product configuration (virtual product testing) as well as a different marketing mix configuration (virtual market testing) in direct collaboration with end-users.

In virtual product testing, the Virtual Reality Markup Language makes it possible to rapidly download images and animation while maintaining high image quality. Consumers can view and evaluate detailed descriptions of each prototype which are integrated with virtual tours around and even inside the product. In this way, all the product components can be seen before consumers make their final evaluation. As in the idea selection stage, consumers can modify, at least in part, some product features by choosing some predefined modular attributes in order to identify the price–attribute combination which best satisfies their individual need. For instance, Google beta-tests its new ideas in the Google Labs section of its website. Web-based beta testing is very common in the software, e-commerce and videogame industries.

This application can also be used to integrate the virtual representation of the product through the reproduction of the other attributes of the marketing mix – from advertising to the representation of the sales force – in order to recreate a total virtual shopping experience. This method, aimed at supporting the market forecast of each product, is called 'information acceleration' (Urban et al., 1996). For instance, in the evaluation of a vehicle prototype, respondents can virtually 'enter' the car, exchange information with other users, interact with the car dealer, view advertising material and so on. One limitation of this information acceleration approach is that a tremendous amount of information is required to reproduce a real simulation of the purchasing experience, so only a few prototypes can be tested in one study.

Finally, it is worth highlighting that conjoint analysis can be used to estimate future market share of prototypes. As Dahan and Srinivasan (2000) demonstrate in a study of the bicycle pump product category, the results obtained from virtual product testing are very accurate, can be carried out at a much lower cost, and are similar to those obtained through physical product testing. This means that this approach can also be used for a variety of durable goods.

Product Launch

The involvement of customers in the NPD process is not going to conclude at the product development stage. Online activities such as communication contests, viral marketing, or web-enabled word of mouth (the so-called 'word of mouse', Reichheld and Schefter, 2000) are tools that can effectively promote products at the stage of product launch (Jurvetson, 2000). Companies can create contests to involve customers in the definition of advertising campaigns. For instance, Ducati and Nikon have encouraged owners of their products to submit snapshots of themselves next to their vehicle (in the case of Ducati) or snapshots that illustrate the power of the camera (in the case of Nikon). These snapshots have then been used in traditional print and TV advertising campaigns, as in the 'Stunning Nikon' print campaign (www.stunningnikon.com). Similarly, Mazda and Conde Nast have partnered to create a contest in which contestants can submit photos that convey their interpretation of Mazda's 'Zoom-Zoom' slogan, while Procter & Gamble, with the initiative 'Pantene Protagonist', has launched a similar competition for its shampoo.

Companies can also promote viral marketing by introducing options such as the possibility of sending a specific web page 'to a friend'. Due to the reliability of the information source, these 'electronic postcards' can enhance both product exposure at a very low cost and product trust (Kenny and Marshall, 2000). Ad hoc incentives – such as discount coupons, free samples or participation in contests – can be offered to both the senders and the recipients of viral messages, in order to effectively support word-of-mouse activities.

This customer-generated marketing communication phenomenon can also be enhanced through virtual communities. Although customer knowledge sharing within a community is less organized and controlled, it is extremely effective since it is based on a spontaneous form of communication. The reciprocal trust catalyzes the exchange of experiences, and vice versa, the exchange of information enhances member relationships (Sproull and Kiesler, 1991). Since users decide to group around a specific area or product category on their own initiative, these communities create a particularly interesting target for the company, to the extent that it is the result of a process of self-segmentation which ensures a high degree of involvement (Hagel and Armstrong, 1997). Therefore, promoting company-run communication activities through forum or chat rooms based on shared values rather than on specific products can considerably influence the purchasing expectations and trends. In fact, users can even turn into evangelists for the company's products. For instance, Apple has benefited from communities such as the www.ipodlounge.com website, where customers congregate to show the world what they would like the next iPod to do and to look like. Similarly, LEGO has greatly benefited from over 50 international virtual communities of LEGO fans, as well as Bricklink.com – the 'Unofficial LEGO Marketplace' created by fans to trade their own products and projects. Going a step further, in 2002, LEGO even offered a new product – the 'Santa Fe Super Chief' – only to its most ardent fanatics, selected through their participation in virtual communities. Without relying on any other commercial investments, LEGO was able to sell the first 10,000 units of this new product in two weeks (Antorini, 2005).

In order to support the launch of new products to targeted groups, virtual communities can be hosted by temporary micro-sites that are created specifically to promote individual product launches. Alternatively, given their strategic importance for the success of the innovation, sites dedicated to new products can be systematically and even permanently set up within the main corporate website, often with links run via the home page. For instance, the over 65,000 members of the self-organized TiVo Community forum use the site Tivocommunity.com in order to trade ideas on how to convince friends and family to buy a Tivo or how to be a better TiVotee.

Customer involvement in the product launch stage can also occur by means of personalized communication, especially newsletters, which focus more on the brand than on the individual product and which are sent to a select group of customers who have opted in to such communication (Godin, 1999). Providing personalized assistance to help customers choose products can also enhance customer relationship management. Companies can organize events, both offline and online, to bring together customers interested in particular new products, and even allow these customers to get a 'sneak peek' at new products that are yet to be launched, to make them feel part of a select group involved in the new product launch. In fact, activities related to customer relationship management and personalized newsletters take on crucial importance throughout the entire new product life cycle. These activities allow the company to systematically interact with its customers and consequently obtain regular feedback so that they can subsequently upgrade the product. Therefore, web-based tools increase the opportunity to make NPD an ongoing process which can benefit from customer input.

3.3   THE ACTUAL USAGE OF THE WEB

The review of the literature has shown how new technologies create the conditions for increasingly closer links between companies and customers, in order to involve the latter as partners in the innovation process. Seminal contributions point out how different tools can enhance each stage of the innovation process (Dahan and Hauser, 2002). We now provide empirical evidence on the actual diffusion of such tools in the websites run by companies operating in five different industries – namely, the automobile, motorcycle, electronics, toiletries, and food and beverage industries – synthesizing the main results already discussed in a previous contribution (Prandelli et al., 2006b).[2] As the purpose was to verify the actual diffusion of web-based tools for collaborative innovation beyond the digital products field, we selected consumer goods industries where continuous innovation is crucial for sustaining competitive advantage, customer knowledge is relevant to enhance the likelihood of success for new products, and digital marketing is gaining increasing importance. Specifically, we built a grid in order to compare the presence of web-based tools of different types and quality.[3] We had two objectives in doing this. First, we wanted to identify the extent to which different companies actually include tools for customer involvement in their innovation process on their websites. Second, we wanted to identify industries where collaborative innovation is more intensively pursued by companies through their own website.

The frequency analyses revealed that companies rely on web-based tools to encourage customer participation more frequently during the early stages of NPD – in particular, during the idea generation stage – and the final stages regarding the product launch and the management of the product life cycle (Table 3.2).

Specifically, during the idea generation stage almost all the sample companies, regardless of the industry, offer consumers the option of a direct contact, and about 37 per cent use the Web to carry out ad hoc surveys or request specific feedback regarding the product or the site. Even the suggestion box, used to collect consumer ideas to improve existing products or launch new ones, is becoming noticeably more important and is now used by 8 per cent of the sample companies. This is a noteworthy development considering the novelty of the tool. In contrast, web-based tools are not widely used during the idea selection stage. The 4 per cent of the sample companies allow individual users to view the evaluations expressed by other customers, regardless of the industry, but there are no direct interactions among the same customers. Totally absent are online focus groups designed to involve customers in the selection of new product concepts. The product design stage relies on a wider range of collaborative mechanisms even though they are still not well established. At the simplest level, input for product design based on customized aesthetic and functional features of the product (3 and 30 per cent, respectively) seems to be a prevailing

Table 3.2   Web-based tools used at the different stages of the product innovation process*

Stage	Tools	Firms using the tool (%)
Idea generation	'Contact the firm' option	90.4
	Feedback session/survey	36.8
	Suggestion box	8.1
Idea selection	Analysis of other customers' opinions	3.8
	Virtual concept test	1.4
Product design	Mass customization of functional attributes	30.1
	Mass customization of aesthetical attributes	2.9
	Patents for new products	1.4
Product test	Complete market test online	24.8
	Virtual product test	0.5
Market launch	New product area	63.2
	Events	49.3
	Customized newsletter	40.7
Product life management	Customized newsletter	54.1
	Customized CRM	32.5

Note: * Because of the still low diffusion of web-based collaboration, we included among the users of a specific web-based tool any player who gets a result greater than 0, considering the index related to the same tool.

Source: Prandelli et al. (2006b).

practice. At a more advanced level, still fewer companies (1.4 per cent) allow customers to submit their patents to develop new products and enter into intellectual property rights agreements. Although the Web is not commonly used during the testing phase of the product, digital environments are commonly considered to verify the overall effectiveness of a particular marketing mix. Almost one-fourth of the sample companies use this tool, especially those operating in the mass-marketed consumer product categories. Finally, a wide range of tools are diffused to support the new product launch and the management of the product life cycle. For instance, it is common to find one area of the site dedicated to informing customers about the history and features of new products (63 per cent); there are also mini-sites dedicated to new products, especially in the electronics (for example, Siemens) and technology (for example, IBM) industries. In addition, the communication of online events, often combined with offline activities (49 per cent), seems to play a key role in promoting the product launch on the market. Customized newsletters, sometimes supported by viral marketing mechanisms, are also commonly used to promote a new product launch (41 per cent), as well as to run the activities related to the following stages of the product life cycle. Numerous other tools are used to perform activities related to web-based customer relationship management (32.5 per cent). Virtual communities, relying on chat rooms and forums, not only promote the spread of product or service information within specific user groups, but also contribute to further reinforcing the customer's tendency to buy. Other mechanisms widely used to support a new product launch are those providing personalized assistance to help consumers select a product. These instruments are often based on model selector or comparison programs designed to allow the user to identify the product – usually electronic (such as a computer: Dell; a television: Blaukpunt; a cellular phone: Nokia; and so on) or automobile (Mercedes, Ford) – which best satisfies their needs. Therefore, within the framework of the growing personalization and enhancement of the interactive features typical of digital environments, the Web plays a fundamental role, especially at the very beginning of the NPD process, during the stage of customer knowledge absorption to generate new product ideas, and at the very end of the same process, during the product launch and life-cycle management stages.

Our analysis of diffusion of web-based tools suggests that they are most commonly spread during the very early or the final stages of the innovation process, especially by companies operating in the toiletries, food and beverage, and motorcycle industries. More precisely, at the earlier stages of the process, the food and beverage, and toiletries companies rely on more traditional tools, such as contact with the company or seeking the opinions of other users. The motorcycle industry, in addition to the traditional instruments, relies on more specific, innovative tools, such as suggestion boxes with copyright regulations, reward mechanisms for new product concepts, and customer advisor programs. The situation is different in the electronics and automobile industries. Companies in these industries rely on web-based tools even in the middle stages of the innovation process involving product development and product testing, especially market testing to assess the market appeal of the finished product. However, although electronics companies are more likely to rely on specific tools in the product development and testing stages (such as consumer patents for new product solutions, open-source mechanisms, product design tools and virtual product tests), automobile companies rely on less innovative tools (such as mass customization and market tests), mainly designed to obtain suggestions from the users indirectly. We also find that the automobile and motorcycle industries are similar in their desire to cultivate customer relations once the product is launched. In this connection, web-based customer relationship management (CRM) tools are widely used in order to enhance the experience for the customer and strengthen his/her loyalty.

3.4 COLLABORATIVE INNOVATION IN PRACTICE: TOWARDS AN EVOLUTIONARY APPROACH

Our empirical survey of over 200 brand and corporate sites shows that web-based tools are still not widely used to improve and accelerate NPD through customer involvement. In fact, collaborative tools are employed only at specific stages of the innovation process, there is a quite limited diffusion of two-way communication tools, and not all companies across industries show the same interest in leveraging these tools.

We find that the diffusion of web-based tools to involve customers in the innovation process tends to be mainly concentrated in the early stages (that is, the stage of the generation of new ideas) and in the later stages (that is, product or service launch and management of the product life cycle). The core activities of the innovation process are instead still controlled and managed by the company. In other words, a growing tendency to 'listen to the customer's voice' through web-based tools is emerging, even if this 'voice' is then reinterpreted and transformed into specific product features through autonomous, in-company activities. Only after the product has been launched does the company go back to using web-based tools for two-way communication and direct customer involvement. In any case, industry specificity tends to play quite a significant role. In particular, the companies in the electronics and automobile industries stand out since at least some of them involve customers even in the most important stages of the innovation process, that is, product development and testing.

In terms of the specific web-based tools used, companies tend to prefer tools that are simply lower-cost versions of the traditional tools they use offline. This suggests a gradual approach where companies can start by initially using web-based tools to replace or enhance traditional tools that they are comfortable with in the offline world, before making the leap to more innovative tools for customer interaction and involvement. These tools include web-based surveys and feedback sessions, newsletters, personalized support for activities related to customer relationship management, and virtual environment events to support the launch of new products and services. Progressively, as companies become more comfortable with and gain more confidence in virtual environments, they can move on to more innovative instruments, especially those designed to support the development stage, such as open-source mechanisms and toolkits to design products. However, note the increasing usage of some new options, such as suggestion boxes and reward mechanisms during the idea generation stage and patents with explicit copyright regulation in the NPD stage. Although these tools are still not widely used, they point the way forward to greater customer involvement in the innovation process, led by industries that develop products with a greater digital content.

In summary, the most common approach to leverage the Web to support collaborative innovation still seems to be incremental, where the traditional activities of NPD are integrated progressively with online tools for systematic customer interaction. Over time, and with experience, we propose that companies can progress towards new tools capable of influencing the process itself and promoting collaborative customer involvement that would be impossible in offline environments. In this context, as we shall see in the next chapter, the most successful development path is to combine a broad set of different web-based tools supporting different stages of the innovation process in an integrated portfolio.

NOTES

1. Copyright © 2006 by the Regents of the University of California, reprinted from the *Californian Management Review*, vol. 48/4. By permission of the Regents.
2. The sample companies were chosen on the basis of their reputation and the markets where they operate: Europe, the US and/or Asia. The survey covered a sample of 209 websites, classified as follows: 35 in the automobile industry (plus 15 sub-brand sites), 14 in the motorcycle industry, 36 in the toiletries industry, 13 multinationals operating in the food and beverage industry (considering in addition about 85 sub-brand sites) and 28 in the consumer electronics industry.
3. Based on the literature analyzed, we identified 28 variables, each designed to describe the specific web-based tools companies can adopt to support the different stages of their innovation process. Each variable was described by a number of different attributes, to make the analysis as objective as possible. Some company performance indexes were developed, which incorporated the information collected in the single attributes per variable we identified. The higher the value of the index, the more the company applies the variable identified at that particular stage. The indexes were created by giving the same weight to each attribute. Each attribute assumed the value of 1 if present and 0 if absent. For each company, the sum of all the attributes considered per variable made it possible to obtain absolute indexes, which were subsequently relativized. Therefore each variable obtained a score between 0 and 1.

4. Managing an integrated portfolio of tools for collaborative innovation

4.1 INTRODUCTION

As we have highlighted in the previous chapter, firms can use a variety of Internet-based mechanisms to facilitate collaborative innovation. These mechanisms differ in terms of the stage of the new product development (NPD) process that they are most useful for. In this chapter, we show how best-practice firms are integrating different mechanisms into a synergistic portfolio.

Specifically, in Section 4.2 we describe how using web-based tools can go beyond their simple association with specific innovation activities. These tools can be combined and modified, taking into consideration the degree of customer involvement they require. We combine a review of past literature and empirical findings with an in-depth analysis of selected case studies to propose a portfolio-based approach for web-based collaborative innovation. We also identify the principal advantages and limitations of each set of tools to sketch out guidelines for companies as they decide which tools to use in their decision-making process.

In Section 4.3 we provide detailed evidence from two case studies of best-practice firms that have successfully implemented an integrated portfolio of web-based mechanisms supporting collaborative innovation – Ducati Motor from the motorcycle industry, and Eli Lilly from the pharmaceutical industry. Finally, in Section 4.4 we discuss the organizational aspects of collaborative innovation. Based on interviews with marketing and information technology (IT) managers from a selected sample of companies, we offer insights into the effective implementation of customer knowledge absorbed through collaborative innovation in the organization. We also explore whether companies are integrating their activities of customer knowledge absorption through their public website with customer knowledge acquired through private websites or through collaboration with independent third parties operating online market research sites. While this analysis is exploratory in nature and we stop short of making sweeping generalizations, we do find some interesting commonalities among the approaches taken by leading companies.

4.2 DEVELOPING AN INTEGRATED PORTFOLIO OF MECHANISMS SUPPORTING COLLABORATIVE INNOVATION

Internet-based collaboration mechanisms can be mapped to the NPD process based not only on the stage of the NPD process at which the customer involvement is desired, but also on the nature of customer involvement that is needed (Sawhney et al., 2005). As we argued in the previous chapter, Internet-based collaboration mechanisms may be classified in terms of their usefulness at different stages of the NPD process: some mechanisms are more relevant at the *front end* of the innovation process – the idea generation and idea selection (concept development) stage; while others are better applied to enhance the *back end* of the process – product design and testing stages. Drawing from organizational learning theory, we can reframe this dichotomy as tools that support *exploration* activities versus tools that support the *exploitation* of new possibilities (for example, Schumpeter, 1934; Holland, 1975). Exploration includes tasks such as search, variation, risk taking, experimentation and discovery. Exploitation implies refinement, choice, selection, implementation and execution. Organizations that mostly leverage the former without the latter suffer the cost of experimentation without gaining many of its benefits, generally exhibiting many undeveloped new ideas. In contrast, organizations engaging in exploitation to the exclusion of exploration risk getting trapped in a suboptimal stable equilibrium. It is important to maintain a dynamic balance between the two approaches to ensure organizational survival and growth (March, 1991). The same considerations can be reinterpreted and applied to virtual settings: integrating the usage of collaborative innovation tools at the front end and at the back end might represent the best way to fully exploit the potential of the Web for exploration as well as exploitation in collaborative NPD.

Turning to the nature of customer involvement, Internet-based collaboration mechanisms can be classified into mechanisms that emphasize *reach* versus mechanisms that emphasize *richness* of the interaction. While the reach versus richness trade-off is not as severe on the Internet as it is in the physical world,[1] it is still a decision that the firm needs to make. The firm may want to emphasize richness over reach if it is mostly interested in generating ideas and insights, enhancing its creativity, and identifying new possible innovation patterns. On the contrary, the same company may value reach over richness if it is especially interested in validating hypotheses with a representative sample of customers, in order to be able to generalize the emerging results and implement concrete actions out of them. Figure 4.1 maps the variety of Internet-based

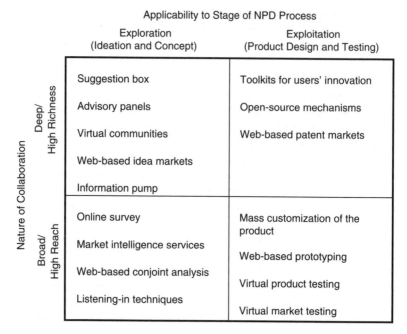

Applicability to Stage of NPD Process

Source: Sawhney et al. (2005).

Figure 4.1 Mapping Internet-based collaboration mechanisms based on nature of collaboration and stage of NPD process

mechanisms we described in Chapter 3 on the two key dimensions we have described.

Mechanisms that are useful to enable deep exploration at the early stages of the NPD process include suggestion boxes where customers can contribute their own innovative ideas, customer advisory panels to solicit customer feedback on a systematic basis, and online virtual communities. Reward mechanisms can also be introduced to encourage the most competent users to compete in Internet-based innovation marketplaces to solve specific problems (Nalebuff and Ayres, 2003). These marketplaces are typically hosted by third parties because of their ability to gather together communities of experts. Examples of such innovation marketplaces include HelloBrain (www.hellobrain.com), Experts Exchange (www.experts-exchange.com), NineSigma (www.ninesigma.com) and Yet2.com (www.yet2.com).

Turning to mechanisms that provide validation at the front end of the NPD process, firms can harness online surveys to get ad hoc customer feedback, online concept labs to test customer reactions to new products that are currently under development, and online market intelligence services that monitor millions of blogs, websites and bulletin boards to identify trends in customer behavior. For instance, firms such as Nielsen BuzzMetrics (www.nielsenbuzzmetrics.com) monitor customer sentiment and consumer-generated media for specific product categories and brands to uncover trends that may be useful for product development. Also, the technique of 'listening in' can be useful at the early stages, as well as the implementations of conjoint analysis tools, in order to get customer feedback from a broad basis of customers in a very limited amount of time and at a very low cost compared to traditional techniques.

Moving to the later stages of the innovation process, deep and rich exploration can be pursued, especially through the usage of toolkits for user innovation and open-source mechanisms, where individual users do not develop the product by themselves – as in the application of customer toolkits at the individual level. Rather, they make small individual contributions to a community-based development effort. Web-based patent markets can also be proficiently applied at this stage. The high level of technical knowledge required from customers in virtual design communities demands that these tools are best applied to engage with a small and carefully selected group of customers who are trend setters or lead users in their specific markets (von Hippel, 2001b).

Finally, validation at the back-end stages of the NPD process is facilitated by mechanisms for testing the product and the marketing mix, exploiting the advantages of low-cost virtual experimentation. These tools include mass customization applications, rapid prototyping and virtual product and market testing.

All these tools are – or at least should be – synergistic and complementary. Moreover, they can mutually reinforce one another. As a consequence, they have to be used simultaneously as part of an integrated innovation strategy, instead of being used as independent 'silos' for dialoguing with customers. We believe that every company should try to combine several mechanisms within an integrated portfolio in order to take advantage of the Web for collaborative innovation most effectively. As summarized in Table 4.1, each tool has specific advantages and can provide specific benefits, but at the same time it also has limitations and constraints. Through a balanced implementation of different mechanisms, firms can create a truly multichannel platform to support their collaborative innovation activities effectively.

*Table 4.1   Mapping Internet-based collaboration mechanisms based on
nature of collaboration and stage of NPD process*

Web-based tools	Advantages	Disadvantages
	Deep exploration	
Suggestion box	Leveraging customer ideas and competences	Risk of unfocused content is time consuming
	Loyalty: it provides individuals with a sense that firms care about what they think and want	Difficulty in transforming the contents into a solution
	Easily supported through incentives	Usage limited to supporting incremental innovation
Customer advisory panels	Cost-effectiveness	Need for continual updating
	Continuous feedback	Great commitment required
	Positive effect on loyalty	
Virtual communities	Enhanced product trust and loyalty	High motivation needed: restricted number of participants
	Leveraging other customer experiences to reduce the perceived risk of new product purchases	Dedicated community managers enforcing participation rules
		Animation costs
Web-based idea markets	Selection of the best customer assets	Participation constraints: time-related, product dependent
	Strong power of incentives	Cost of payoffs and intellectual property rights management
Information pump	Eliciting and comparing information from a large number of dispersed customers at the same time	Group-thinking phenomena
		Management costs
	Broad exploration	
Online survey	High versatility (opportunity to get feedback on site, product, services)	Sample control
		Self-completed questionnaires
	Limited costs and real-time feedback to reduce uncertainty	Predominance of pre-codified items
Market intelligence services	Up-to-date information on a broad basis	Front-end focus only
	Low-cost monitoring in real time	Need for dedicated organizational resources
		Investments in developing the

Table 4.1 (continued)

Web-based tools	Advantages	Disadvantages
	Opportunities to uncover new marketing trends	same language of the target group
Web-based conjoint analysis	Interfaces which are enjoyable to be navigated	Different results when different configurations are used
	Easy to implement	Time consuming for the customer
	Definition of the product attributes interaction and their ideal combination	
Listening-in techniques	Increased customer satisfaction	Need for collaborative filtering applications
	Time-purchase decision reduction	Dedicated organizational competences
	Affective commitment	
	Incentive for 'parking' on website	

Deep exploitation

Toolkits for users' innovation	Access to sticky customer knowledge	Translating user designs into inputs for production
	Learning-by-doing process	Need for user-friendly technologies
	First-mover advantages	High development cost
	Contribution to radical innovation	
Open-source mechanisms	Reciprocal relationship in creating a high-quality product	Clear participation rules and incentives needed
	Flexibility	Modular project structure
	Knowledge sharing and integration	Undirected innovation and potential chaos
	Enhancement of user reputation	Low internal coordination
	Sense of group responsibility	
Web-based patent markets	Completely developed new product	Property rights recognition
		Patent management
	Original and quality-certified ideas	

Broad exploitation

Mass customization of the product	Easy to implement for the firm	Product modularity needed
	Useful to enhance the customer experience	Technological competences
	Opportunity to define ideal	Usage for incremental

Table 4.1   (continued)

Web-based tools	Advantages	Disadvantages
	combinations of attributes	innovation only
	Enhanced customer loyalty through personalization	No access to customer competences
Web-based prototyping	Close access to single-product features	Limitations for touch and feel products
	Useful to enhance the customer experience	Need for highly interactive interfaces
	Real-time feedback	
Virtual product test	Response flexibility and possible changes in market and technology reducing product development time	Product-related limitation: not all products can be virtually tested
		Lack of sensory experience
	Learning from low-cost mistakes	Technology constraints: limited bandwidth
	Multimediality	
Virtual market test	Low cost of simulating product use	Great amount of information required to reproduce a simulation of the purchasing experience
	Estimating future market share	

4.3   PUTTING THE PORTFOLIO OF WEB-BASED MECHANISMS TO WORK: THE EXPERIENCES OF DUCATI MOTOR AND ELI LILLY

Ducati Motor

In the motorcycle industry, companies create a competitive advantage based not only on technical product superiority, but also on their ability to interact with their customers and create deep customer relationships across the entire life cycle of ownership. Motorcycles are a lifestyle-intensive product, so motorcycle companies need to foster a sense of community among their customers in addition to offering innovative product features[2].

Ducati Motor, a manufacturer of motorcycles headquartered in Italy, was quick to realize the potential for using the Internet to engage customers in its NPD efforts. The company set up a Web division and a dedicated website – www.ducati.com – in early 2000, inspired by the Internet sales of the MH900evolution, a limited-production motorcycle. Within thirty minutes, the entire year's production was sold out, making Ducati a leading

Applicability to Stage of NPD Process

	Front end (Ideation and Concept)	Back end (Product Design and Testing)
Deep/ High Richness	Tech Cafe Advisory programs supported by product engineers Ducati Service Technical Forum & Chat	Design Your Dream Ducati Focalized contest Ducati Garage Challenge Virtual teams
Broad/ High Reach	Online survey to improve the Web site Polls & feedback sessions MyDucati Virtual scenarios	Mass customization of the product Web-based product testing

(left axis label: Nature of Collaboration)

Source: Sawhney et al. (2005).

Figure 4.2   Ducati's Internet-based collaborative innovation initiatives

international e-commerce player. Since then, Ducati has evolved its site to create a robust virtual customer community that had almost 200,000 registered users by the end of 2006. Community management has become so central at Ducati that management has replaced the words 'marketing' and 'customer' by the words 'community' and 'fan'. Ducati considers the community of fans to be a major asset of the company and it strives to use the Internet to enhance the 'fan experience'. Ducati involves its fans on a systematic basis to reinforce the places, the events and the people that express the Ducati lifestyle and Ducati's desired brand image. The community function is tightly connected with the product development, and the fan involvement in the community directly influences product development. Ducati uses web-based mechanisms to support rich as well as broad customer engagement, at the front- as well as at the back-end stages of its product development process (Figure 4.2).

Virtual communities play a key role in helping the company to explore new product concepts. Ducati has promoted and managed ad hoc online forums and chats for over three years to harness a strong sense of community among Ducati fans. Over 200 messages are posted every day on Ducati forums. The most popular discussion is about products and the biking experience. These conversations are highly relevant for Ducati to better understand customer needs and gain insights into new products and services. Ducati also realized that a significant number of its fans spend their leisure time not only riding, but also in maintaining and personalizing, their bikes. As a result, Ducati fans have a profound technical knowledge that they are eager to share with other fans. To support such knowledge sharing, the company has created the 'Tech Café', a forum for exchanging technical knowledge. In this virtual environment, fans can share their projects for customizing motorcycles, provide suggestions to improve Ducati's next-generation products, and even post their own mechanical and technical designs, with suggestions for innovations in aesthetic attributes as well as mechanical functions. To support their ideas, they can attach text or graphics files. In the customer service area of the website, individual bikers can self-signal their technical competences and solve mechanical problems posted by other Ducati fans. These technical forums help Ducati to benefit from spontaneous customer knowledge sharing, and help the company to glean suggestions for improving its marketing engineering and customer support.

Being deeply aware about the possibilities of the Web, in March 2006, the CEO Federico Minoli started his own blog – 'Desmoblog' – within Ducati.com, to promote 'creative chaos' in the virtual environment. This is the first corporate blog in the motorcycle industry worldwide. It has been created without any form of censorship and it has been used to improve NPD and launch on the final market. For instance, in the spirit of 'opening the gates of the factory', some months before the launch of the new motorcycle Hypermotard, in May 2007, Minoli started to post a series of comments directly involving the customers in the final stages of the product development process. Examples of this series of comments are a video clip on You Tube, the purpose of which was to bring the fans 'behind the scenes of the Research and Development department to see first hand where the Hypermotard is today, to see how things are being put into place and to hear the impressions of the test riders who have ridden the bike' (Federico Minoli, Desmoblog, February 14, 2007). The three-minute video showed the prototype of the bike being tested, first in the factory and then on nearby roads. One week later, on February 21, 2007, a second video was posted, showing the first test of the Hypermotard on the Mores circuit, together with a telephone interview with the pilot in charge of the test, who talked about the performances of the prototype. The aim of these initiatives was not only to keep customers informed and to create a 'Hypermotard fever', but also to be true to the disruptive spirit of the bike by creating communication in which 'we eliminated any kind of exclusivity, and we will build up the launch directly on the Internet, starting from me riding the bike in the hills around Bologna', according to Minoli.

While not all fans participate in the online forums, those who do provide rich inputs for exploring new product concepts and technical solutions. These forums also help Ducati to enhance customer loyalty, because its fans are more motivated to buy products they helped to create. Ducati's CEO has mandated the involvement of all the company's product engineers in customer relationship management activities. They are required to periodically interview selected Ducati owners from the company's online database of registered fans – adding a physical dimension to the online interaction. Ducati also attempts to go beyond its customer base in an effort to gather ideas from as broad an audience as possible. Ducati community managers monitor relevant forums and bulletin boards hosted on independent websites, such as the community of American Ducati fans hosted on Yahoo!. Ducati community managers take part in these forums, sometimes identifying themselves and remaining anonymous at other times, based on the nature of the topics and the sensitivity of the audience to privacy concerns. Ducati managers also monitor vertical portals created for bikers, including Motorcyclist.com and Motoride.com, micro-sites that gather specific segments of interest to Ducati's. These include sites that list women bikers – the fastest-growing demographic group in motorcycling – as well as 'girl-friends, wives, and mothers of Ducati fans'. In addition, Ducati monitors other virtual communities that have lifestyle associations with the Ducati brand. For instance, Ducati has entered into a partnership with the apparel fashion company DKNY to tap into their community and interact with their members. Through these diverse 'listening posts', Ducati tries to ensure that it expands its peripheral vision beyond its own customers, and beyond the customers it can reach directly by itself.

The ideas and insights that emerge from the mechanisms we describe are rich and creative, but they do not necessarily represent the preferences of the broader market for Ducati products. To validate its insights, Ducati uses online customer surveys to test product concepts and to quantify customer preferences. As a testimony to the ability of Ducati to create both an ongoing customer dialogue and a sense of engagement with its fans, Ducati gets extraordinary response rates, often in excess of 25 per cent, when it surveys its customers. Ducati uses customer feedback for activities that go beyond product development. The layout and functions of Ducati's website are shaped by customer feedback, and the guests for live chats on the site are also chosen based on customer input.

For instance, on October 20, 2003, three new concepts of Ducati SportClassic were presented simultaneously at the Tokyo International Motorshow and online with a mini-site from which it was possible to access an ad hoc survey. The purpose was to understand the interest of the public in the motorcycles in order to decide whether to proceed and if so, which one to put into production; in fact, no engineering components had been developed at that time. On the website, consumers were asked to fill in a questionnaire, either signing into the Ducati website as a community member or registering quickly, providing only a few socio-demographic details such as e-mail, country, age and gender. The questionnaire was divided into three sections related to the three models, and a final section with more generic information about the individual fans. The product-related sections aimed at investigating four main issues for each of the three models. First, Ducati asked customers to identify the most intriguing aspects in very general terms (for example, design and style, technical aspects, classic heritage, riding position, riding pleasure, dimensions, or anything else) and the features to be improved (for example, color scheme, engine and a list of design elements). Second, the survey asked the consumers whether Ducati should produce the motorcycle and their willingness to purchase it. Almost 15,000 answers were collected in five days, and more than 96 per cent of them recommended the production of all three models. In total, over 310,000 people visited the SportClassic site and more than 16,000 took part in the survey, expressing enthusiasm and interest in Ducati SportClassic. As a consequence, the company decided to put all three models into production, and to launch them on the market sequentially, so that the Paul Smart 1000 Limited Edition was released first (November 2005), followed by the Sport 1000 (March 2006) and then the GT 1000 (September 2006).

To encourage customers to participate in online surveys, Ducati has created a sophisticated incentive system based on both tangible and intangible payoffs. For instance, every week Ducati launches a competition called 'Name the picture', in which participants have to guess what part of the bike an image shows to enter the 'Hall of Desmohead-Fame'. In these events, technical knowledge becomes a passport to enter a highly qualified virtual community of fans.

Ducati's new website, which went online in September 2004, features a new registration form where fans can share personal information about their experience with Ducati motorbikes and allows them to provide suggestions for accessories that can complement the biking experience. Similar features are also provided on the customized MyDucati pages that each fan can create and personalize.

Ducati also pursues Internet-based customer collaboration at the back end of its innovation process. Virtual communities play an important role at the product design and market testing stages. For instance, in early 2001, the community managers of Ducati.com identified a group of customers on its website who had particularly strong relationships with the company. They decided to transform these customers into active partners, involving them in virtual teams that cooperate with professionals from the R&D, product management, and design departments of Ducati Motors. These virtual teams of customers work with the company's engineers to define attributes and technical features for the 'next bike'. Through this mechanism, Ducati recognizes opinion leadership and provides recognition for members within its customer community. Contests are also used in order to enhance and reward customer involvement. For instance, in 2002 the company created a competition called 'Design Your Dream Ducati', where fans were challenged to interpret in any form their 'Dream Ducati'. The contest asked customers to be creative around the theme of Ducati passion. Customers were asked to submit a design project for a new Ducati motorcycle (one's dream Ducati) or any kind of artistic interpretation of the Ducati world (one's Ducati dream), as a representation of one's personal way of living the passion around the Ducati world. The response rate was incredibly high, and the winning projects were selected by a team involving, among others, the CEO, the Chief Manager of the Design Department, the Creative Director, and some journalists. Hence, this event was also an occasion to directly involve a traditional R&D department in online activities in the light of the undergoing Dotcom integration.

Future contests will focus on specific areas of interest for the company, including soliciting solutions to specific mechanical and aesthetic problems – a form of web-based 'idea market'. The company also plans to integrate its online and offline mechanisms for customer engagement. For instance, during the World Ducati Week (WDW), an annual gathering in Italy of Ducati fans from all over the world, the company organizes the Ducati Garage Challenge. The purpose of this gathering is to allow bike owners to show how they transformed their Ducati based on their skills and creativity. At the 2004 gathering, more than 20 motorcycles constructed by Ducati were remodelled through the imagination of customers who worked in the Ducati workshops to transform their dreams into reality. The winners are selected through votes cast by official Ducati riders, as well as by the company's technical and styling directors.

Notwithstanding the origin of the 'next bike', all new product designs are reviewed and tested with a broader sample of customers. Ducati's fans can surf thousands of pages illustrating the mechanical features of Ducati motorbikes. Within the virtual community, current and future Ducati bike owners discuss and review proposed product modifications that can be tested online in the form of virtual prototypes. They can even vote to reject proposed modifications. They can also personalize products to their own preferences, and can ask Ducati technicians for suggestions on personalizing their bikes. To answer such questions, the Internet division relies on technical experts within the company.

Eli Lilly

The pharmaceutical industry relies heavily on innovation to sustain competitive advantage. The average cost of discovering and developing a new drug is more than $500 million, and the average length of time from discovery to patent is 15 years. Eli Lilly, an Indianapolis-based pharmaceutical firm, has created an Internet-based platform to support collaborative innovation involving its customers – patients, doctors, clinicians, researchers and healthcare providers. The company employs more than 35,000 people worldwide, and markets medicines to treat depression, schizophrenia, diabetes, cancer, osteoporosis and many other diseases in almost 140 countries. Like its competitors, Eli Lilly invests heavily in R&D, consistent with the philosophy of its founder, who referred to research as 'the heart of the business, the soul of the enterprise'.

In recent years, the company has sought to make its innovation processes more widely distributed by leveraging the Internet. In the late 1990s, the company created a new division – e.Lilly – dedicated to using the Internet to manage customer interactions with the explicit purpose of supporting R&D activities. e.Lilly focused on engaging potential creative partners, including customers, in a dialogue to explore new ideas and strategies for growth. It aimed to create new and unanticipated connections among patients, doctors and employees, because these connections facilitate creative solutions to innovation problems. e.Lilly is responsible for two main streams of web-based activities – generation of new drugs and creation of new patient solutions. Each stream of activities is pursued through a specific website and ad hoc mechanisms of customer engagement, selectively applied at the early and later stages of the innovation process (Figure 4.3).

In order to collaboratively explore new solutions to problems of patients suffering from diseases, the company invites them to participate in specialized forums where they can socialize their experiences and share advice. Ad hoc forums allow the medical community and patients affected by the same pathologies to engage in a shared experience of learning about a specific health condition, while providing useful insights to the company in order to creatively drive its idea generation process.

To enhance its validation activities at the front end, Lilly educates and involves patients on a broader basis, through the corporate website (www.elililly.com) and its direct links to related websites, such as the Lilly Centre for Women's Health (www.lillywomenshealth.com). Patient

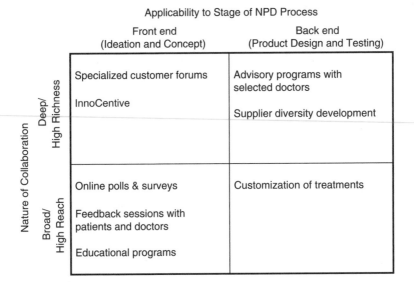

Source: Sawhney et al. (2005).

Figure 4.3   Eli Lilly's Internet-based collaborative innovation initiatives

involvement in therapy is enhanced through customized information offered on the Web and feedback sessions. The purpose is to empower patients to choose their personal treatment options by providing them with information about diseases as well as potential therapies. At the same time, Lilly is able to generate valuable feedback about new product concepts from a representative sample of customers through online polls and surveys.

Eli Lilly also uses the Internet as a platform for involving scientists in the innovation process by directly engaging them in innovation-related problem solving. The company has created a venture called InnoCentive (Innovation + Incentive) that functions as a web-based market where solutions to problems are traded and participation is enhanced through competitive problem solving. The purpose of InnoCentive is to enable collaboration with lead users and communities of experts who have expertise to solve innovation-related problems. InnoCentive posts scientific problems to be solved by qualified scientists, without regard to geography, time zones or background. The InnoCentive.com website encourages scientists to find problems that match their qualifications and then work independently or collaborate to find the best solution. InnoCentive allows Eli Lilly to engage experts from around the world on a contingent basis to facilitate its R&D efforts. It has been spun off as an independent company, and it has broadened its mission to acting as an independent third party that connects 'solvers' with 'seeker' companies in a variety of industries including biotechnology, agribusiness and consumer products.

A key issue in facilitating customer involvement in innovation is the design of appropriate reward mechanisms for customers. In the case of InnoCentive, scientists are offered cash rewards that are explicitly defined on the website. Scientists work and submit solutions with the understanding that only the best solution will receive the financial award. InnoCentive is a cost-effective, convenient and speedy mechanism for Eli Lilly to tap into the broad and rich base of distributed knowledge among the world's scientists. It allows Lilly to expand its scientific R&D capacity without adding to its employee costs.

To understand the power of this Internet-based distributed innovation platform, consider an example of an innovation challenge – to improve the manufacturing process of a chemical called 4-(4-hydroxyphenyl) butanoic acid. After Eli Lilly's internal R&D organization had spent 12 man-months of work on this problem, the result was a five-step process that needed expensive starting materials and produced low yields. The goal was to devise a two-step process that had a starting cost of less than $100 per kilogram and produced a better yield. The problem was posted on InnoCentive's site in June 2003. It soon received several submissions, including a promising approach suggested by Werner Mueller, a retired senior scientist from Hoechst Celanese. At the end of November 2003, Mueller's fifth submission was accepted and he was awarded $25,000 by InnoCentive. In less than five months, one scientist had solved a problem that had eluded a team of researchers at Eli Lilly. By early 2007, InnoCentive had signed on 120,000 scientists and scientific organizations from more than 175 countries competing to solve research challenges with awards ranging up to US$1,000,000. InnoCentive has also signed up several companies including BASF, Dow Chemical and Procter & Gamble to post scientific problems confidentially on the InnoCentive website.

Eli Lilly also engages its customers at later stages in the NPD process. Doctors are engaged through advisory programs aimed at supporting continuous feedback on specific solutions to selected pathologies, in order to better anticipate market evolution and identify the most appropriate period to launch a new treatment on the market. An extension of these programs has led to the supplier diversity development (SDD), aimed at broadening participation of minority and women-owned businesses – often managed by the same company's clients, such as researchers and clinicians – in the Lilly supplier base to levels more reflective of the diverse business community. In addition, patients are involved in customizing the treatments and therapies the company provides them based on their preferences and the specifics of their disease conditions. The basic drugs can be the same, but the therapy is personalized case by case to reflect individual history and experience.

4.4   THE ORGANIZATIONAL SIDE OF COLLABORATIVE INNOVATION

Until this point we have primarily focused our attention on the tools that companies can include in their website in order to support collaborative innovation with customers. However, tools are not enough to ensure the effective usage and implementation of the outcomes of collaborative innovation. As the two best-practice case studies revealed, deep organizational changes have to be implemented in order to put into practice the knowledge acquired at the front end and transform it into concrete inputs for NPD. To shed light on the organizational issues surrounding implementation of collaborative innovation, we integrated our previous considerations with information gathered through direct interviews with marketing and IT managers from a selected sample of companies.

Our purpose was twofold. First, we wanted to understand whether companies are integrating their activities of customer knowledge absorption through their public website with activities of customer knowledge acquisition through private websites or through the collaboration with independent third parties operating market research online. In other words, we wanted to understand whether companies are integrating a 'make' option in web-based customer involvement for innovation with a 'buy' option. Second, we wanted to gain insights into organizational mechanisms that are essential for the effective implementation of imported customer knowledge within the innovation process. We caution that this analysis is truly exploratory in nature, and we have no ambition of generalization. Our findings suggest that outsourcing strategies in customer knowledge absorption for innovation appear to be taken into consideration, especially by companies that also intensively use their own website, both in its public and private versions, to collaborate with customers. Cooperation with independent operators running research online seems to be pursued usually to extend the objectivity and the scope of the collected information. In most cases, the imported inputs are then partially implemented.

For instance, BMW Auto effected a reorganization to support an effective usage of customer knowledge that it absorbs through the Web. It created a new function called 'customer prospect relationship management' (CPRM) that is responsible for both customer relationship management and proactive marketing strategies. Responsibilities related to Internet-based market research have been reallocated from the marketing to the CPRM function.

The Web is intensively used to absorb customer inputs and to profile users in order to develop customized commercial initiatives. Interactive mini-websites are often created to support the launch of specific new products. The content developed online by customers through interactions – both in the company's websites and in independent communities spontaneously created by the same users – is systematically analyzed by specific roles within the CPRM and then selectively distributed to individual departments according to contingent needs. The marketing department pays considerable attention to feedback that comes in through the Web from innovative customers, and this feedback is then verified on larger and more representative samples of customers through traditional market research tools.

In the fast-moving consumer goods market, P&G has created an organizational structure to support customer involvement in innovation, in both traditional and virtual environments. The Global Business Unit at the headquarters is responsible for the core Web strategy, but the market development organization at the local level can interpret it according to its market context and needs. This unified approach has resulted in every website becoming more customer- than brand-centered. The company started to leverage the Web in the 1980s, but it is only since 2001 that it has been using virtual environments to involve customers in the innovation process. Interactive tools in the public version of individual websites are used to collaborate with customers at both the idea generation and the product launch stages, leveraging virtual communities, virtual marketing initiatives, and two-way communication to enhance its brands. Online surveys and suggestion boxes – to solicit both advice and complaints – are extensively used. Customer feedback gathered online is systematically integrated with information collected through traditional call centers, which remain the most important channel for hearing the customer's voice. Virtual concept tests are hosted in private areas of specific websites, where only a pre-selected group of 'lead' or 'trendsetter' customers can participate and provide feedback. In order to support the market test and the product launch stages with a broader set of customers, P&G cooperates with market research firms running their own websites. Interfunctional meetings and informal brainstorming activities – involving marketing, R&D and customer market knowledge – are then organized to share the customer inputs internally. The company considers these activities to be strategic, because both customer satisfaction and competitive advantage are enhanced when customers are involved in the innovation process.

Similarly, Nestlé uses its own public corporate and brand websites to consolidate its image and create a dialogue with its customers, while specific concept tests are run through private websites protected by passwords that are managed by independent research institutes, where the Nestlé logo does not even appear, in order to not influence the customers' answers. The Web strategy is defined by the Nestlé customer relationship management function, which is in the process of reorganizing the institutional site around topics such as health and nutrition, in order to enhance opportunities for interactivity and improve customer profiling. In this way, the Web helps the company enrich its customer database, which is then used to select customers that can be contacted via e-mail and involved in specific market research initiatives.

Kraft Foods, the largest branded food and beverage company in North America, is convinced that the Internet is progressively becoming an important part of building consumer relationships and driving business success. Recognizing the importance of importing the customer's voice and sharing it within the organization for sustaining its competitive advantage, Kraft has started leveraging the potentialities of virtual environments by using its brand websites for developing more interactive communication: asking customers not only how good its products are but also how they would like them to be (for example, the Recipe Connection on the Kraft Interactive Kitchen website). The company also cooperates closely with independent third parties that can support the company's NPD process at the front as well as at the back end. For instance, Kraft works with online research firms such as ComScore Networks (www.comscore.com) to better understand its consumers' shopping behaviors and needs. The information provided by ComScore enables Kraft to measure the effectiveness of its online efforts.

The systematic integration of information collected through the corporate website with information gathered by research institutes is also common to high-tech companies such as Siemens. Within its website, the company uses surveys and suggestion boxes to collect customers' complaints, such as in the troubleshooting area, where customers can identify the model of their cell phone and share the specific problems that they have faced while using it. This content is then analyzed by Siemens, together with the customer feedback obtained via e-mail, in order to discover possible solutions. Beta-testing activities are also often centrally developed online, while open-source mechanisms and contests are applied within both the global website and its local versions, especially for Java applications. The emerging solutions suggested by customers are then implemented, although problems in managing intellectual property rights limit the extent to which peer-to-peer tools can be used by Siemens in NPD.

Nokia is another example of a company that has integrated its traditional mechanisms for absorbing customer knowledge with more innovative ones, such as cooperation forums and online communities. Through Forum Nokia – an online community created to bring together professional developers working with technologies and platforms supported by Nokia mobile devices – the company promotes open standards that match its customers' needs. This program connects developers with tools, technical information, support and distribution channels to build and market applications around the globe. In order to implement the ideas from these collaborative open mechanisms, Nokia reorganized into four platforms: mobile phones, multimedia, networks and enterprise solutions. The purpose was to give potential growth areas both greater exposure and flexibility, ensuring that new products match the overall vision. Each division acts like an incubator, where actors are free to imagine new products or services taking root. Ideas flow faster, since individuals have more opportunities for contact with customers, and an 'essential market insights' group is tasked with steering customer insights towards product development. To extend the scope of these insights, cooperation with market research institutes running ad hoc websites is selectively pursued.

In summary, this exploratory analysis suggests that specific organizational mechanisms are needed to implement the customer knowledge absorbed through the Web for enhancing innovation. Firms need to systematically support customer knowledge distribution across departments and across geographies based on their specific needs. Specific organizational roles can be created to this end. Companies that have started to include tools enabling customer collaboration in NPD within their own websites seem to be aware that the Internet is an easy-to-use global medium with unprecedented reach. For this reason, leading firms are pushing towards a 'make' option in web-based customer collaboration for innovation. At the same time, such companies also appear to be more willing to integrate customer knowledge directly absorbed through their own websites with customer knowledge provided by independent third parties operating online. They also pursue a 'buy' option to extend the scope of customer insights by leveraging information collected by online research operators to interact with a category of consumers that is broader than their regular customer base, in order to gain unbiased feedback.

While the scope of insights can be expanded through ad hoc collaboration with third parties, we are witnessing a broader move towards open and externally focused innovation approaches that rely on harnessing the creativity of a wide variety of dispersed actors. This distributed approach to innovation is the focus of the next chapter.

NOTE

1   See Chapter 2 for a detailed analysis about the opportunities to overcome the reach–richness trade-off in virtual settings.
2. An earlier version of this case and the following one were described in Sawhney et al. (2005).

5. From collaborative to distributed innovation

5.1 INTRODUCTION

One of the managerial advances that have resulted from the widespread deployment of ICT is the ability to greatly enhance a firm's innovation capacity by leveraging *external* knowledge resources beyond individual customers. While the importance of absorbing external knowledge to support innovation has been understood for some time (for example, Cohen and Levinthal, 1990; Zahra and George, 2002), firms have historically been limited in their ability to reach beyond their boundaries for innovative ideas. This limitation is the result of a variety of factors, including the absence of open standards for communication and the idiosyncrasy of knowledge (Arora and Gambardella, 1994). Consequently, the interorganizational division of innovative labor has traditionally been limited to a few specialized industries such as biotechnology (Shan et al., 1994; Powell et al., 1996), pharmaceuticals (Cockburn et al., 2000), and the automotive industry (Langlois and Robertson, 1995; Dyer and Nobeoka, 2000).

This situation has begun to change dramatically with the emergence of the Internet as an open, global and ubiquitous platform for communication. The Internet has opened new doors to firms seeking to create new organizational mechanisms to support their absorptive capacities. Enhanced connectivity through the Internet allows different actors in the markets to become contributors and collaborators in innovation (Iansiti and MacCormack, 1997; Prahalad and Ramaswamy, 2004). Internet-enabled virtual environments offer firms new avenues to interact with suppliers (Thomke and Kuemmerle, 2002). Web-based communities enable a highly decentralized approach to innovation activity involving large numbers of independent contributors.

It is important to note that this opportunity comes at an opportune time as it addresses the emerging need of firms to augment their knowledge and capabilities in a world where knowledge is widely distributed and deeply specialized; this means that companies cannot afford to rely entirely on their own employees for ideas and insights (Chesbrough, 2003). In addition, internal inventions not being used in a firm's business need to be taken outside the company (for example, through licensing, joint ventures and spinoffs).

In this chapter, we investigate the emerging phenomenon of distributed innovation – namely, the activities in support of innovation involving a division of labor among independent and geographically dispersed actors that are enabled by ICT. These independent actors can be other firms, communities of customers, or third-party organizations. The rest of this chapter is organized into four key sections. First (Section 5.2), we provide a basic taxonomy of distributed innovation that identifies the key players – that is, communities of creation, virtual knowledge brokers and open-source systems. Then we provide an overview of the key characteristics of each of them (Sections 5.3–5). Finally, Section 5.6 summarizes.

5.2   A TAXONOMY FOR DISTRIBUTED INNOVATION MECHANISMS

The literature on distributed innovation has emerged at the intersection of several functional disciplines, including marketing, technology, R&D management and organization science. To organize our understanding of the literature, we identify two key dimensions to classify the various forms of distributed innovation mechanisms that can be crossed to create a two-by-two matrix (Figure 5.1). The first dimension is the *form of governance* of the innovation process. Some scholars who have studied the process of distributed innovation assume a firm-centric model, where a single firm is the central actor, and it creates connections around itself with customers or

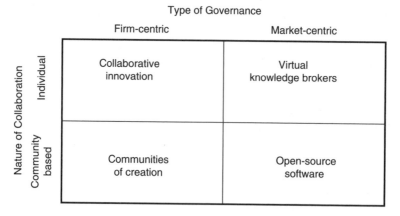

Figure 5.1   A framework for classifying models of distributed innovation

partners. Other authors take a market- or community-centric perspective. In this case, the locus of the innovation process is the market itself, and the innovation mechanism emerges organically as independent actors come together to collaborate. The second dimension is the *nature of collaboration* between the actors that contribute to the innovation process. Some distributed innovation mechanisms focus on a traditional form of collaboration, where the firm collaborates with actors in the market (customers, suppliers or partners) on an *individual basis*. Other mechanisms involve a *community approach*, where it is the web of relations among the different actors that becomes the focus of attention.

By crossing these two dimensions, we arrive at four key mechanisms for distributed innovation:

- collaborative innovation;
- communities of creation;
- virtual knowledge brokers; and
- open-source systems.

In the remainder of this section, we review the characteristics and functions of each mechanism, and derive implications for managing distributed innovation.

While collaborative innovation mechanisms reflect what we have already learned in the first chapters of this book (the idea is that firms can create superior products and services by collaborating with individual customers in the process of creating new products and services), we now focus our discussion on the three quadrants of the matrix pertaining to communities of creation, virtual knowledge brokers and open-source systems.

5.3 COMMUNITIES OF CREATION

The community-centric model shifts the locus of innovation beyond the boundaries of the firm, to a community of individuals and firms that collaborate to create joint intellectual property. This model relies on the well-known idea that knowledge is socially constructed (for example, Schmitt, 1994; Nonaka and Takeuchi, 1995; von Krogh and Roos, 1995; Goldman, 1999), so knowledge creation can be significantly enhanced through participation in 'communities of practice' (for example, Brown and Duguid, 1991; Wenger, 1998). While communities of practice do not have to be Internet based and the idea of communities of practice predates the Internet, such communities have traditionally been considered mechanisms to catalyze situated (Lave and Wenger, 1991) and distributed (Sproull and

Kiesler, 1991) learning within the individual organization, in some cases serving as an alternative to teams (Wenger and Snyder, 2000).

Virtual communities of practice focus on new knowledge creation, called 'communities of creation', which allow the social creation of knowledge to extend far beyond the boundaries of the firm. The community of creation is a governance mechanism for managing innovation that lies between the hierarchy-based (closed) mechanism and the market-based (open) mechanism for innovation management (Sawhney and Prandelli, 2000a). It blends the benefits of hierarchies and markets by offering a compromise between too much structure (in a hierarchy) and complete chaos (in a free-for-all market). It overcomes the lack of coordination typical of markets, while emphasizing the contribution to a shared project of all contributors. Within the community, explicit as well as tacit knowledge can be shared because participants build up a common context of experience, allowing them to socialize knowledge developed in specific contexts (Nonaka and Konno, 1998).

This mechanism seems particularly relevant at a time when knowledge is the main source of economic rents, and new knowledge is being created at a furious pace. Today's turbulent markets demand speed and flexibility, variety and cohesiveness. They also demand collaborative knowledge creation with players that are outside the direct control of the firm. In such a context, the focus shifts from minimizing transaction costs for the individual firm (Williamson, 1985) to maximizing transactional value created by networks of firms, in order to increase the 'net present value of exchange relationships' (Zajac and Olsen, 1993). Thus, interorganizational strategies – extended also to customers – that have greater joint value may be more effective in order to enhance the potential for innovation, even though they may involve the use of less-efficient governance mechanisms from a transaction cost perspective. To this end, instead of designing rules that embody fixed decisions, the firm needs to act as a coordinator, designing rules that enable flexible decision making, as in the 'agoric open systems' originated in the software industry for collaborative software creation (Miller and Drexler, 1988).[1]

In order to function effectively, a community of creation requires a specific set of ground rules for participation. A key challenge is to create incentives for participation and cooperation within the community by recognizing the contribution of any actor who shares his/her knowledge assets (Kozinets, 1999). To preserve a semblance of order, a coordinator is also needed, as well as screening mechanisms to avoid misleading contributions. The community of creation functions like a 'gated community', where residents move about freely inside the community, but only if they satisfy some pre-specified access rules. The governance structures for a community of creation are informal, but this does not necessarily mean that they are weak (Hagel and Singer, 1999). In some cases, control can be based on restricting access to the best information assets. The community also needs a sponsor who defines the architecture and the standards around which the community is organized. The sponsor facilitates the interaction, and ensures that the emergent organization is both efficient and effective. Finally, a system for managing intellectual property rights is required (Thurow, 1997). To favor cooperation in knowledge creation, the property rights of *ideas*, and not only of their *expressions*, have to be recognized. New mechanisms are needed to take into account the fact that the most innovative ideas are often the output of a joint process, within which it is difficult to discern the specific contributions of single actors. As a consequence, intellectual property rights vest in the community that creates innovation, instead of belonging to individual contributors within the community. The community-centric innovation model is more democratic than the traditional hierarchical innovation model because it empowers peripheral players, giving them the right to contribute their own experiences and individual knowledge to the final output (Sawhney and Kotler, 2001).

5.4 VIRTUAL KNOWLEDGE BROKERS

Virtual knowledge brokers (VKBs) are the virtual manifestation of knowledge brokers – third parties who connect, recombine and transfer knowledge to companies in order to facilitate innovation (Hargadon and Sutton, 2000). While firms can improve innovation by engaging directly in virtual environments, they need to augment *direct* virtual connectivity – namely, self-managed virtual environments – with *mediated channels* that can facilitate innovation (Verona et al., 2006). In the physical world, knowledge brokers take the form of innovation and design consulting firms (Sutton, 2002; Hargadon, 2003). In the virtual world, however, such brokers are more diverse, the scope of their activities is broader, and their potential impact on the innovation process can be greater. VKBs are firms that operate in virtual environments and play a knowledge-brokering role that involves absorbing both market and technical knowledge to support innovation. Internet-based brokers such as CNET.com, Homestore.com and Edmunds.com have evolved into VKBs in the technology, home ownership and automobile markets, respectively, by gathering information on industry-specific products and organizing communities of interests around these industries. Building upon their initial role of information intermediaries or 'Infomediaries' (Hagel and Singer, 1999), they are evolving into innovation intermediaries or 'Innomediaries' (Sawhney et al., 2003). VKBs gather dispersed individual and collective knowledge, and distribute it to firms after organizing and elaborating it to support innovation. Firms are interested in this knowledge for at least two different reasons. First, they are constrained by their cognitive limits and their core competences (Leonard-Barton, 1992), and their peripheral vision often does not extend beyond their served markets. Second, their reach is physically limited by geography and industry boundaries (Sawhney et al., 2003). By working on a global and interindustrial basis, VKBs can greatly enhance the reach and richness of connections between firms and actors who can provide knowledge to support innovation.

The activities of VKBs are characterized by four key processes: (a) network access; (b) knowledge absorption; (c) knowledge integration; and (d) knowledge implementation. Through network access, VKBs have access to new forms of knowledge that might interest a third party for innovation purposes. The VKB's ability to extend the web of relations with different actors in the market improves the effectiveness of network access. The second process refers to knowledge absorption. After accessing the source of new knowledge, a VKB needs to internalize this knowledge and make the knowledge its own. This internalization requires it to possess an absorptive capacity (Cohen and Levinthal, 1990). The third process deals with knowledge integration, which allows the new absorbed knowledge to be combined with existing knowledge and stored in the VKB's organizational memory. Finally, knowledge implementation helps the VKB to deliver the solution to the customers that it serves. Network access is strongly amplified by the Internet and its ubiquitous reach. The Internet's unique properties also positively influence the processes of knowledge absorption, integration and implementation.

5.5   OPEN SOURCE SYSTEMS

Open-source systems (OSS) represent a specific evolution of virtual communities, completely run by and for users to mutually provide technical advice (Constant et al., 1996) and create new products or services (Kogut and Metiu, 2001; von Hippel, 2001; von Hippel and von Krogh, 2003). They are based on the joint development of knowledge and innovation brought into being by several independent individual actors. In open-source programs, individual users do not have to develop everything they need on their own, but can benefit from the freely shared contributions of others.

In order to understand the OSS innovation model, it is important to briefly trace its origin. OSS originated in the software industry, where many thousands of free and open-source software products have been created over time (for example, Fielding, 1999). The history of OSS dates back to the early days of computer programming (Raymond, 1999). Initially, software development was carried out independently or jointly by technicians on a free basis. The knowledge needed to develop and maintain software was difficult to come by, so when individuals needed a specific bug fix or an upgrade, they developed the practice of freely giving and exchanging software they had written. This became a part of the 'hacker culture' (von Krogh and von Hippel, 2003). However, it was a major event that gave rise to the birth of an official movement: the creation of a new license called GPL (General Public License) by Richard Stallman, a scientist at MIT's Artificial Intelligence Laboratory. Stallman found it offensive that software developed throughout this 'open' practice was then licensed to a company for commercial release, thereby limiting the opportunity to use it as a platform for further development (Moody, 2001). He went on to establish the Free Software Foundation with the specific objective of developing a legal mechanism that would allow software developers to preserve the free status of the software by using a specific copyright that would grant a number of rights to future users (von Krogh, 2003). These rights imply that any user may obtain a copy at no cost, and then legally study its source code, modify it, and distribute it to others, also for free (Lakhani and von Hippel, 2000).

Some time during 1998, the name of the movement changed from 'free' to 'open' software, because this more accurately reflected the intent of the movement – open access to innovation. The OSS movement took off after this point, fuelled by the growth of the Internet as a global medium to connect actors participating in OSS projects such as Linux and Apache (Kogut and Metiu, 2001). By 2003, more than 10,000 OSS projects involving more than 300,000 individuals were in progress (von Krogh, 2003).

The OSS model is a fundamental advance in the management of distributed innovation, because it is an open model that contrasts significantly with the traditional proprietary or closed model of managing innovation (Chesbrough, 2003). The openness and inclusiveness of the OSS model makes it far less susceptible to the limitations of closed innovation models, including self-referentiality, limited resources, and natural limits on skills that a single firm can garner under one roof. In order to allow the OSS mechanism to work effectively, some important conditions have to be met (von Hippel, 2001). First, at least some users must have sufficient motivation to innovate, that is, the expected benefits of innovating should exceed their costs of participation. Second, at least some users should have an incentive to voluntarily reveal their innovations and the means to do so. Finally, user-led diffusion of innovations should be able to compete with commercial production and distribution, often through for-profit firms which provide installation, maintenance and support services that complement the open-source products. In fact, it was not until large commercial players such as IBM, HP and Intel put their support behind open-source software products such as Linux that the OSS ecosystem really started to take off. These technology giants contribute technology, marketing, complementary products and software professionals to the Linux ecosystem. IBM alone has 600 programmers dedicated to Linux, and almost 90 per cent of all contributions to Linux come from programmers who work at for-profit technology companies (Hamm, 2005).

The conditions that must be satisfied to sustain OSS require more investigation in future research along many dimensions. First, the system of incentives to contribute to the process of innovation has not been clearly articulated. Some authors suggest that career incentives can provide an important stimulus to contribute to the process (Lerner and Tirole, 2002; von Hippel and von Krogh, 2003) and enhancement of one's own reputation and expectations of reciprocity. Furthermore, the combination of commitment to the group and the awareness of affecting the environment can represent powerful incentives (Kollock, 1999). However, much remains to be done to define reputation-based incentives more precisely. Second, the evolution pathways for the governance of OSS projects are still unclear. For instance, the Linux ecosystem, while very decentralized, had until recently been very tightly and dictatorially controlled by Linus Torvalds, the author of Linux. More recently, the governance has been delegated to a community called Open Software Development Labs (OSDL) and a team of experts overseen by Torvalds. This change in governance suggests that as OSS projects become more global, more complex and more commercially important, some elements of hierarchy may need to be introduced into the community-based governance model to prevent the fragmentation of the community. Third, even if OSS mechanisms have been extended beyond the software industry to other industries involving the development of physical products, such as in the sportswear industry (von Hippel, 2001), the OSS model is still largely confined to the software industry. The OSS model seems to be less viable for contexts where components of a new product cannot be created, delivered and assembled over the Internet. This may represent an important limitation that needs to be overcome for the adoption of the OSS model in different industries.

5.6   THE GOVERNANCE CONTINUUM OF DISTRIBUTED INNOVATION

In Table 5.1, we summarize the four different mechanisms for distributed innovation and provide a summary of the key properties of these

Table 5.1   Models of distributed innovation

	Collaborative innovation	Communities of creation	Open-source systems	Virtual knowledge brokers
Governance Collaboration	Firm-centric 1-to-1	Firm-centric Community based	Market-centric Community based	Market-centric 1-to-1
Incentives of collaboration	Early access to new products, influence over innovation, economic incentives	Reputation and passion	Career; reputation	Specific fees
Type of outcome	Data and competences through self-designed products	Insights or specific knowledge for innovation	Chats ('free talk') or products ('free beer')	Specific codified knowledge for innovation (e.g., patents, licenses, products)
Type of interaction	Spot, based on the firm's contingent needs	Continuous, based on ground rules for participation	Spot or continuous, based on individual available competences	Spot or continuous, based on the network of firms' contingent needs
Examples	P&G Siemens,	Ducati, Sun Microsystems	Linux, IBM Alphaworks	Innocentive; Yet2; TechEx
Limitations	Knowledge from individual customers	Bias of the firm as community coordinator	Public knowledge, industry specificity	Knowledge delivery

mechanisms. The main differences among the mechanisms arise from two dimensions that define their identity, namely the type of governance and the type of collaboration. For instance, the type of knowledge they help generate may range from unstructured information and ideas for innovation to completely developed solutions. The interaction needed to support the creation of such knowledge can be episodic or sustained, depending upon the firms' needs and the customers' competences. Further, the

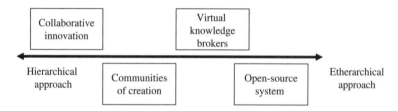

Figure 5.2   The governance continuum for models of distributed innovation

incentives offered to contributors may also be different across the mechanisms. Opinion leadership and reputation may be adequate payoff to stimulate participation in OSS and in communities of creation, where the sense of belonging is a significant motivator. More concrete incentives may be required to stimulate involvement in value co-creation and virtual knowledge brokerage activities, where participants may want something of tangible value in return for their participation.

An important implication of these considerations is that each mechanism supports different types of innovation and in different ways. Therefore, the different mechanisms complement one another. Hence, a firm that wants to pursue competitive advantage thorough innovation on an ongoing basis should employ a portfolio of such mechanisms to overcome limitations of specific mechanisms.

The four models also present different elements of governance and are characterized by different degrees of involvement of external actors (Prandelli et al., 2006a). Based on this distinction, we can arrange them along a continuum from hierarchical to etherarchical approaches (Figure 5.2). Models of co-creation are characterized by a strong degree of autonomy and hence can be considered analogous to hierarchical models typical of the classic approach of innovation management. The more we move to community-based models – from communities of creation to VKBs and OSS – the more the mechanism looks like an etherarchical approach, characterized by emergent and unplanned behavior. In the chapters that follow, we analyze in more detail these community-based models, beginning with communities of creation.

NOTE

1. An agoric system is a software system using market mechanisms, allowing for software to be distributed across and to serve different owners pursuing different goals. The proponents of agoric systems argue that decentralized planning is potentially more rational, since it involves more minds taking into account more information. However, the agoric

system is more complex than classic decentralization, because decentralization has to be combined with a central direction of resource allocation. Therefore, a hierarchical structure remains the basic governance mechanism for coordinating knowledge socialization processes, but these processes are fed and catalyzed by the contribution of the market for transaction types that are not effectively supported within hierarchical organizations (Miller and Drexler, 1988).

6. Virtual communities

6.1 INTRODUCTION

In this chapter, we examine the emerging phenomenon of virtual communities, which is playing an increasingly important role in the distributed innovation process. The Internet has meaningfully and irreversibly changed the way relationships are created and promoted with and among consumers. Consequently, firms have no choice but to develop interactive channels of communication with communities of customers.

The Internet lends itself very well as a forum for forming and growing communities, because, at its heart, the Internet is a social medium. It has a decentralized structure with no hierarchical organization, so it allows peer-to-peer conversations to develop without any centralized control. A hallmark of the Internet is its ability to aggregate specialized resources without regard to geography. Increasingly, knowledge diffused on the Web tends to regroup spontaneously around shared interests in the search for affinities and reciprocal enrichment. Specialized knowledge within a specific cluster of people tends to combine with socially generated knowledge between different clusters, permitting learning from very different industries and domains to be synthesized. As such, the Internet has become fertile ground for the germination and growth of communities that combine creativity, knowledge and competences of individual contributors.

We open the chapter with some observations on the meaning of the term 'virtual community', and we identify contexts within which the concept can be applied. Then, we focus on virtual communities of consumption. In particular, we point out how important it is for firms to strategically manage these communities to maximize their contribution to product innovation. We examine the function of virtual communities of consumption as tools of distributed learning, and we highlight the social and experiential dimension of consumer knowledge. We conclude by observing that virtual communities will find more acceptance as tools for market sensing as well as tools to support new product development.

6.2 MEMBER PROFILES AND ENVIRONMENTS

Despite their economic and productive applications, virtual communities are first and foremost *social* groups (Jones, 1997) that share cognitive, emotional and material resources (McAlexander et al., 2002). At a social level, they represent the 'connective tissue' of networked communities now revitalized by the proliferation of weblogs – 'blogs' created by individuals to stimulate discussions on subjects of personal interest that currently attract 75,000 new members every day.[1] The first virtual community, the Well, was established at the end of the 1980s and headed by Howard Rheingold. It started as a dialog between the writers and readers of the *Whole Earth Review*, and evolved over the last two decades into one of the world's most influential online communities. The Well's message reflects the essence of networks: it epitomizes the profound social connections that the Internet can create between people (Hagel and Armstrong, 1997). Rheingold, credited with coining the term 'virtual communities', defined them as 'social aggregations that emerge from the Net when enough people carry on public discussions long enough, with sufficient human feeling, to form webs of personal relationships in cyberspace' (Rheingold, 1993). This first definition therefore refers to:

- a size element: there has to be a minimum critical mass of users to make the community attractive;
- a temporal element: interactions cannot be occasional contacts; and
- an element of conscious participation that is crucial to developing a sense of belonging.

Although the definition is very generic, it highlights a number of phenomena, underlining the fact that the Net is a space where people can freely communicate their values and interests, and presents the opportunity to meet and carry on conversations with no restrictions. This definition was subsequently applied to so many different online social groups that it gave rise to a heated academic debate regarding the conditions that make a virtual community a 'real community' in the traditional sociological sense of the term (for example, Garton et al., 1997; Paccagnella, 1997; Liu, 1999; Wellman and Gulia, 1999). This debate stems from the conviction that most relationships in digital environments are characterized by scant commitment (Watson, 1997) and the communication is less rich due to the absence of the non-verbal component (for example, Sproull and Kiesler, 1986). In actual fact, the key components of traditional communities – the sense of belonging, sharing the same rituals, the sense of moral responsibility – can often be found on the Net (for example, Kozinets, 2001; Muniz and

O'Guinn, 2001; Bagozzi and Dholakia, 2002), and building emotional relationships and sharing emotions are not necessarily inhibited by computer-
mediated communication (for example, Walther, 1992, 1995). However,
transposing these components to the digital environment will depend on
the type of community. In particular, the ones von Hippel (2005: 96) calls
'innovation communities', namely, 'nodes consisting of individuals or firms
interconnected by information transfer links which may involve face-to-
face, electronic or other communications', do not necessarily have all the
traditional components of communities.

Virtual communities can aggregate different kinds of members, from the
collaborators of a single firm that access information from their Intranet
networks, to extended communities, suppliers and distribution partners
that develop from the interconnection between different Intranets – the so-
called 'corporate Extranets' – to communities that develop in the open
Internet environment, aggregating users who share the same interests and
want to share their experiences by building a common background.
Although we mainly focus on the third type of community, it is worth
noting that the first two can also contribute interesting ideas to support
innovation.

Intranet communities deal mainly with innovative projects such as
'Knowledge Management', which aims to better organize, diffuse and
memorize the knowledge that the firm's internal contributors have accumulated over time in order to optimize processes without having to continuously find the solution to the same problems and to prevent the firm from
losing its knowledge capital when there is a turnover in personnel (for
example, Fahey and Prusak, 1999; Hansen et al., 1999). In particular, the
creation of a 'Knowledge Catalog for Knowledge Retrieval' allows companies to develop a kind of mapping and classification system of the knowledge resources distributed within the organization, creating semantic links
between them so that they can be easily retrieved. Similarly, the development of Knowledge Management Intranet allows the firm to enhance the
professional communities within the organization and recognize individual
information needs. Intranets allow groups to form spontaneously and cut
across the corporate hierarchy. People can converse freely, discuss their
ideas, exchange information, and thus develop new ideas that would otherwise remain unexpressed (Davenport and Prusak, 1998).

Extranet communities are vertical, sectorial aggregations that aim to
promote better communication between operators who belong to the same
industry and are interested in promoting the exchange of information and
products. They often become virtual *marketplaces* that provide forums for
members to interact. These communities extend the channels of communication and transactions beyond the boundaries of the firm. There is a

growing tendency for large, multinational companies to physically and geographically decentralize their planning, design, research and experimentation activities to virtual environments in order to enhance distributed competences and enable rich low-cost connections between firms belonging to the same value network (Upton and McAfee, 1996). Virtual communities create relational ties that extend beyond the firm's boundaries, representing a new way of dividing cognitive work (Orlikowsky, 1992) among numerous subjects who share the same language and the same relational ties, despite the absence of a space–time proximity. Since it is possible to substitute physical connection between operations and operators through information networks, firms can adopt more flexible architectures that can easily be redesigned every time different subjects are involved, depending on the specific development needs of new processes or products (Rullani, 1997; Gambardella and Rullani, 1999).

The common interest of a community in a particular subject can vary depending on whether it is a community of practice (Brown and Duguid, 1991; Wenger, 1998; Hildreth, 2004) or a community of knowledge (Boland and Tenkasi, 1995). Communities of practice aim to promote socially generated experiences that members often develop in the context of a single firm and later in a broader context. In this way, they create shared knowledge that can be reused and becomes embedded over time. These communities help firms improve management strategies, pursue new lines of business, identify and retain the most talented people, develop personal competences, easily transfer best practices, and solve internal problems more rapidly (Wenger and Snyder, 2000). For instance, there is a community of people who repair Xerox photocopiers. When solutions are found to specific problems, they can be accessed by customers abroad (Brown and Duguid, 2000). Another example is the community of Sears employees and partners who share their most successful experiences in managing distribution channels and evaluating the experiences of colleagues by means of a rating system linked to the company's incentive system.

Communities of knowledge tend to develop a common worldview based on the opinions exchanged by all the participants and the knowledge of individual members. This is the case of most communities that spring up around fashion or social phenomena. These communities offer interesting opportunities to interact with consumers, obtain feedback in real time, and produce new products by working directly with end users. In fact, these end users are no longer isolated actors since they can aggregate in communities that give importance to the opinions of individual members. By aggregating individual customers into groups, virtual communities are beginning to play a key role in empowering consumers, as firms cannot afford to ignore the opinions of large organized customer groups.

6.3   KEY CHARACTERISTICS OF COMMUNITIES OF CREATION

A virtual community of consumers is made up of a network of individuals who engage in a distributed process of knowledge creation in a computer-mediated environment. The typical development model of the relationships within this community tends to combine consumer knowledge and social interaction (Walther, 1995), in a pattern where mere exchange of information evolves over time into connections that become socially 'thicker' and stable. However, enduring relationships do not necessarily become consolidated among all the community members. The strength of these ties usually depends on the importance the user attributes to the consumer activities around which the community revolves, and on the intensity of the social ties that are created between community members. Based on these dimensions – relationships with the consumer activity and relationships with the virtual community – it is possible to build a matrix that identifies four types of participants (Kozinets, 1999): the tourists, who do not develop strong ties with the group and are only superficially or temporarily interested in the consumer activity; the minglers, who maintain strong social ties but are only minimally interested in consumer activity; the devotees, who manifest the exact opposite behavior; and finally the insiders, who manifest strong social ties and equally strong personal ties with the consumer activity. From the perspective of distributed innovation, firms are most interested in developing systematic and ongoing interactions with the last two types of participants. Moreover, preliminary research shows that the 'thicker' and more loyal consumers in virtual communities are in fact represented by devotees and insiders (ibid.). Therefore only with these participants can a particularly rich fabric of relationships develop between the firm and the consumers and among the consumers themselves.

In order to precisely differentiate virtual from physical communities, besides the mechanism of transmitting information, it is important to reflect upon the differences between the two. First, there is a fundamental difference in the method employed to develop shared knowledge. Physical communities are formed on the basis of a common territorial, historical and value matrix, usually rooted in a common religion (Jones, 1997) that aims to protect and reinforce the knowledge built within the community in order to sanction the members of the group. Conversely, virtual communities tend to act as mechanisms that continually regenerate accumulated knowledge. The socially generated experiences of new members are emergent and unpredictable, which means that the community's embedded knowledge capital is continually adapted and modified. The larger the community, the more participants are inclined to contribute and thus expand the knowledge capital. This also implies that while a physical community has clearly recognizable boundaries and a univocal definition of its members, the boundaries of a virtual community are continually changing, mirror the contingent search for new forms of knowledge that new members can bring, and reflect the participation rules that members help define and develop (Wallace, 1999). Therefore, the creative potential of the virtual community is greater, although building reciprocal trust between members is obviously more complicated since there is no physical interaction and the composition of the community is fluid and continually changing. Moreover, even the level of involvement tends to be different since unlike many physical communities, online communities are made up of members who decide to belong to such a group. For example, one automatically belongs to a local community for reasons of birth or residence, but the decision to participate in a discussion group is always a deliberate choice (Prandelli and Verona, 2006). Moreover, since the registration process simply requires completing a form and is not particularly binding, it is not particularly significant when joining a community. In fact, people who adhere to various online initiatives do not feel that they belong to a large number of communities. Other elements have to come from 'below' – that is, from the participants – and from 'above' – that is, from the community managers – for there to be a real community of consumption.

A central element in the formation of a community is a collective identity with which the community members can identify. A community can survive over time only if it is based on trust and fosters a sense of identification and belonging. It is this social identity together with the positive feelings that the users can anticipate that makes them want to participate in a virtual community (Bagozzi and Dholakia, 2002). However, the social identity is not necessarily the starting-point of a community. Although in some cases, the social ends might have been clearly defined by the founders, in many others the group that was spontaneously formed around an initial stimulus led to the emergence of common viewpoints, values that came to be gradually shared, and ad hoc social structures that little by little shaped the real 'personality' of the community (Micelli and Prandelli, 2000). In the best cases, a similar process even generates specific social rituals or group behavioral norms (Postmes et al., 1999), as well as a reference language or a semantic system open to the construction of shared meanings (Di Bernardo and Rullani, 1990) that enhance the intellectual capital of a particular community and its story.

While this sense of collective identity and trust based on a sense of belonging are crucial to the emergence of a viable virtual community of consumers, it is not enough to ensure its existence. Scholars who have studied the rise of online communities emphasize the importance of the original material that participants contribute (Hagel and Armstrong, 1997). In order to establish a vibrant virtual community of consumers, there has to be a distinctive model of interaction that integrates in a synergistic way the communication between members and member-generated content. Integrating content-generation and shared experiences based on reciprocal trust and on the sense of belonging is of fundamental importance in forming and sustaining virtual communities.

A revolutionary consequence of communities is the fact that isolated consumers, once considered passive recipients of corporate communications, can now coalesce into groups who regularly exchange ideas, information and experiences. They often pool their competences and even give rise to forms of resistance when corporate practices are perceived to infringe upon their rights (Kozinets and Handelman, 1998). Virtual communities have given consumers power that was unimaginable just a few years ago.

6.4   DESIGNING AND MANAGING A COMMUNITY

There are at least five key functions that an important virtual community can carry out for a firm:

- aggregating demand on a global scale;
- market research;
- intensifying the flow of communication with and between consumers;
- co-defining the values associated with the brand; and
- fostering user loyalty.

In fact, apart from some exceptional cases, not all virtual communities carry out the five functions simultaneously. Different types of communities can carry out different functions and support different stages of the innovation process (Table 6.1). As shown in greater detail in the discussion that follows, to truly make virtual communities of consumption into real tools of shared learning and insights, it is important to create communities that combine the five functions listed above.

The first key function of virtual communities of consumption is to aggregate demand on a global scale. Communities mitigate the difficulty of making trade-offs between the phenomena of global consumption – the idea that consumers, irrespective of their culture and location, purchase and enjoy the same products – and the phenomenon of fragmented product preferences and the search for customized products. In other words, these

Table 6.1   Functions of the virtual communities of consumption, typologies and role in the innovation process

Function	Typology	Role in the innovation process
Aggregation of the demand on a global scale	Community of consumption that supports transaction processes	Testing new product concepts
Market research	Community of interest	Concept generation and selection
Intensifying the flow of communication with and between consumers	Community of relationships	Product market launch
Co-defining the values associated with the brand	Community of relationships and fantasy	Concept generation and product market launch
Fostering user loyalty	Community of interest and community of relationships	Management of product life cycle

communities can recreate online global or extra-national segments for highly customized consumption and allow like-minded, geographically dispersed consumers to meet in virtual environments for even the most exotic products and issues. The implication for firms is that, by enabling voluntary membership around highly specialized common interests, virtual communities of consumption can reverse the problem of segmentation since the consumers themselves are required to define the firm's offerings. The reversal of the segmentation process takes place by self-signalling and self-segmentation by customers. This reverse segmentation is important because it helps firms to solve one of the most complex and crucial marketing problems for a successful new product launch – identifying the target audience. It also fosters the creation of segments of customers that have a high level of involvement and therefore are more willing to participate in the firm's initiatives (Kim, 2000; McAlexander et al., 2002). This type of function is usually carried out by the virtual communities of consumption that support transaction processes. These communities are created on the Web for the specific purpose of facilitating e-commerce operations, to make it easier to buy and sell products and services, as well as transfer information to their own associates (Hagel and Armstrong, 1997). Therefore, there can be communities that aggregate subjects interested in consulting each other before making a purchase in a given product category or communities that group together consumers willing to jointly engage in a commercial transaction, for example, to obtain low prices. This is the case of purchasing groups that offline are only involved in industrial markets and on the Net are also present in consumer markets (Hagel, 1999).

The second important function of communities is allowing firms to better understand customer needs. In fact, firms now have the opportunity to gain access in real time to an authentically social and experiential dimension rooted in the context of use (Lave and Wenger, 1991), consumption knowledge that is particularly relevant in sectors where the significance – and consequently the value attributed to the product offered – depends on the values associated with it through mechanisms that give it a collective meaning (Wenger, 1998). This often occurs in the case of fashionable upmarket products. Using virtual consumer communities as a special tool to do market research can help develop products that satisfy collective needs. New qualitative research methods based on content analysis of virtual community interactions are emerging. One such method is netnography. This technique adapts ethnography to the study of virtual environments and studies the behavior of online consumer groups by applying the techniques of social anthropology to member-generated products (Kozinets, 1998, 2002).

Consider how the apparel company Diesel uses communities to understand its customers. It has created its own community websites where consumers are urged to express their opinions regarding the collections and the Diesel lifestyle. In addition, it also monitors conversations on sites that transmit the biggest traffic to its own sites, in order to expand the scope of its 'listening posts' (Sawhney et al., 2003). For instance, it pays close attention to consumer-generated content in the best-known music and entertainment sites that closely match Diesel's target audience. Moreover, since firms realize that traditional focus groups are not enough to provide insights into customers' unarticulated needs, they can create dedicated micro-sites to back individual communication campaigns in order to see how consumers react to specific issues. Consumer feedback from these micro-sites can be re-aggregated reprocessed and transferred to the corporate divisions that might be interested.

In general, market research is done by the so-called 'communities of interest', which are aggregations of individuals determined to study areas of common interest, exchange information on specific issues, update themselves, and continuously enrich their respective knowledge to be better equipped to also deal with offline activities. In this case, the reputation of the community depends on the breadth and updated content of the site as well as the quality of member contributions, the presence of specialized experts, and the creation of events with competent guests (Hennig-Thurau et al., 2004). These types of communities tend to develop around categories of interest closely linked to the profession of the members or around issues they feel strongly about; the degree of emotional involvement is as high as their specific technical competence.

A third key function of virtual consumer communities is to redesign the flow of communication between firms and consumers that used to be one-way, namely, from the firm to the consumers. In community environments, communication tends to be on equal terms, a move towards 'information democracy' (Sawhney and Kotler, 2001) where all the members have the right to access the same information, participate in a collective dialogue, and thus actively contribute to generating content that augments the common knowledge capital. The implications of information democracy are far-reaching. Consumers expect to have updated, detailed information about the firm and its products, and they want to be actively involved in marketing decisions regarding the firm's products. They want to be able to express their opinions and even their complaints through 'word of mouse' (Reichheld and Schefter, 2000) which, if not immediately addressed, could damage the firm's image as perceived by those who have no information or previous experience (Chatterjee, 2001). Therefore, for the first time, the firm is in a position to monitor in real time the word of mouth between consumers, namely, the marketing phenomenon that influences the speed and success of a new product launched on the market (for example, Johnson Brown and Reingen, 1987; Herr et al., 1991) and that is much more powerful on the Net (for example, Bickart and Schindler, 2001; Rothaermel and Sugiyama, 2001). The word-of-mouth phenomena have increased thanks to the so-called 'communities of relationships', made up of participants determined to create a fabric of robust interactions with other Net users who want to experience the virtual environment as space for meaningful social exchanges. The real identity of the individual often plays such an important role that these communities become tools to create contacts that subsequently develop into offline relationships. Therefore, in this case, more than the breadth of knowledge and the quality of the competence, what really matters are personal experiences and the desire to share them with other users who have nothing to gain from hiding their real identity (Laing et al., 2004). Generally speaking, this process of socially generated experiences can also help mitigate doubts regarding an important purchase, especially when the individual finds it difficult to forecast benefits without having tried out a product beforehand, as in the case of experience goods. In this case, the community can contribute significantly not only during the concept-generation and selection stage, but also by facilitating the product's market penetration.

Another function of virtual communities is to collaborate with the firm in promoting processes that define not only the product itself but also the values associated with the firm's brands. In other words, consumers can be actively involved in creating the brand message by engaging in discussions regarding the brand's meanings (Muniz and O'Guinn, 2001). The shared experiences of the community members can be transformed into an input that can enhance and develop the values associated with a given brand consistent with the development trajectory followed by its users. Therefore, instead of the corporate image being imposed by top management (the top-down approach) there is a growing tendency to allow consumers to collaborate in the process (the bottom-up approach). In this perspective, it is the interaction of the users themselves that allows the real brand messages to emerge. The users can enrich the firm's product according to guiding principles that are often not predictable beforehand, but that, for this very reason, make the users identify even more with the brand (McWilliam, 2000). The firm therefore has to engage the consumer at the start of its activities and processes, triggering a virtuous cycle that sees the consumer as 'activator and recipient' in a collaborative process (Bardakci and Whitelock, 2004) – in other words, the party who benefits and at the same time shapes the values associated with a brand through the dynamics of a social matrix where the community acts as a catalyst.

In addition to the communities of relationships, others that can help co-define the corporate brand are the so-called 'fantasy' communities, which give more importance to interaction and ongoing dialogue than to specific competences. The members emphasize interaction in order to expand the virtual environment rather than competing to gain more power within the community (Beaubien, 1996; Reid, 1999). In this case, what matters is not the real identity of the participants, their specific background, or the quality of their knowledge, but instead the desire to create new environments and stories, take on a virtual identity, and augment it over time in order to live in a world that parallels the real one. This imaginary world has its own rules, its own social circles, and its own ways of enhancing one's personal reputation within an imaginary world. Fantasy communities can help firms to consolidate the collective experience of their customers, to allow customers to overcome the fear of expressing themselves, eliminate barriers that prevent their customers from expressing tacit knowledge, and explore through games the less rational and sometimes more intimate aspects of their personality and behaviors that they would otherwise be reluctant to express (for example, Galimberti et al., 2001; Warisse Turner et al., 2001).

Virtual communities of consumption can also build customer loyalty by continuing to enhance and consolidate the firm's perceived value by participating in the activities promoted by the firm. In this way, barriers are created to prevent the consumer from leaving the relationship with a given firm that are directly proportional to the utility the consumer associates with the firm and with the entire ecosystem of peer-to-peer relationships (Okleshen and Grossbart, 1998). If the user decides to stop interacting with the firm and its community, he/she loses all the relationships within the community. The more specific the language of a given community and the stronger the sense of identity the community arouses, the greater the price of abandoning the community. In other words, the organization of virtual communities increases the *stickiness* of the user site and fosters the development of positive attitudes that can further support *brand loyalty* (Holland and Baker, 2001). In the end, the collaborators become involved in managing the product throughout its life cycle. From this standpoint, communities of interest as well as communities of relationships can play a key role in helping improve the profile of the individual users and making it difficult to replace their contributions.

Only if the virtual communities of consumption manage to combine the five functions described in a synergistic way can they promote a truly collaborative learning process with the reference market. They can act as a catalyst and make the firm's entire innovation process more effective, thereby accelerating not only the concept-generation and selection stage and product launch but also the development of the product itself (Sawhney et al., 2005). The innovation process can be made even more dynamic by enhancing the specific technical competences of the consumers within a virtual community that are rooted in the experiences of the users. Moreover, by monitoring and actively participating in consumer communities run by competing firms and in independent communities that are proliferating on the Net, it is possible to absorb stimuli and extend the learning potential even further. The process of collaborative innovation can involve consumers who are distant – and therefore unbiased – from the *core* competences developed by the firm and, consequently, capable of uncovering more *disruptive* solutions. Therefore, different typologies of communities have to be simultaneously governed in order to absorb different kinds of market knowledge that can boost the firm's new product development process (Figure 6.1).

An example of a fruitful utilization of a virtual community of consumption as a tool of collaborative innovation is provided by the videogame industries that offer 'beta' versions of their product, namely, almost definitive versions of the product, to game-oriented communities – their own fans and independent ones – so that the beta versions can be tested and programming errors reported. The competences of the users of these communities are often so sophisticated that not only are errors reported, but solutions are also generated, thus considerably reducing the firm's time to market and product quality. Texas Instruments, for example,

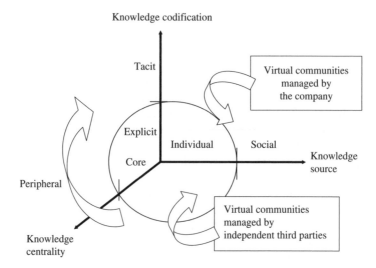

*Figure 6.1　Virtual communities of consumption as a distributed learning
　　　　　　tool: towards an integrated community portfolio*

worked with several virtual groups of educators to develop a new line of
pocket calculators for elementary and high school students. It supported
the creation of a community called T3 (Teachers Teaching with
Technology) to understand the needs of the teachers, evaluate the new
models, and test them in simulated classes in virtual environments.

A virtual community of consumption can play this role only if certain
conditions are met. The community has to be able to creatively integrate the
information dimension within the community. This dimension is linked to
the quality of the competences of the participants and the quality, precision
and depth of the information exchanged – as in communities that support
transactions and in communities of interest. It also has to be able to integrate
the participatory dimension that is dependent on the degree of interaction
among the members – as in communities of relationships and communities
of fantasy. Moreover, this community has to manage these two dimensions
so that they can mutually reinforce each other over time. Therefore, by bal-
ancing the information component and the relational–emotional one, the
virtual community can be transformed into credible learning tools that firms
can depend on. The community can thus overcome the traditional logic of
the market and create the conditions for a new economy based on participation rather than mere transactions, on sharing rather than exploiting
resources in order to obtain the best results for only one of the parties
involved. Only virtual communities of consumption that can maintain this

dynamic balance can fully actualize their potential as learning communities (Micelli, 2000).

Not all the communities of learning seem to be created with this lofty goal in mind. However, irrespective of gradual adjustments that have to be made, only under these conditions can virtual communities of consumption represent an effective response to the problem of how to increase the rate of innovation and develop new products that can better satisfy customers as they have always profitably done. This is exemplified by the case of Ducati, which has been quite successful due to the invaluable contribution of its virtual community of fans as described in Chapter 4.

In order for the community members to participate in an innovation process in an environment where it is difficult to identify the contribution of individual members, there must be complete trust in the firm that coordinates the community as well as in the other community members (for example, Shankar et al., 2003). Trust tends to be reinforced over time through repeated interactions, resulting in progressively stronger community relationships (Sproull and Kiesler, 1991).

The best way to foster trust in a given firm is to implement transparent communication policies (Balasubramanian et al., 1998), and adopt some kind of division of the payoff, in order to prevent the perception of relational opportunism (Prandelli and von Krogh, 2000). Reciprocity represents the fundamental rule of online interaction (Wellman and Gulia, 1999). Trusting in a community is influenced by two key factors. First, there have to be suitable mechanisms that can corroborate information that is deliberately distorted. This is exemplified by the Ciao.com community where users can enter and earn money that is subsequently deposited in their account. They have to either express their opinions regarding a number of product categories and brands according to predefined parameters or evaluate the opinions of others. The case of eBay is another well-known example. It has more than 60 million members who evaluate the trustworthiness of the network's individual sellers. The members' activities have given rise to a distribution system worth over $53 billion and representing an entire parallel universe of commerce.

Another way of fostering trust in the relationship is represented by the benefit the individual continually receives from the other community members (Hennig-Thurau et al., 2004). This is exemplified by the software industry. The time that the users spend on the Internet trying to identify possible bugs in software products and coming up with fixes is strongly influenced by the number of users involved in the process and by the kind of solutions proposed. In this case, trust is mainly fostered by reputation, by the legitimate recognition of belonging to a restricted group of users with particularly refined capabilities that gain prestige and recognition for their specific competences within the community (Okleshen and Grossbart, 1998).

To sum up, in order to trigger a process of distributed learning, the development model of the virtual communities of consumption has to be based on some cardinal principles that, in turn, impact the firm's managerial and organizational structure as shown in Table 6.2 (Sawhney and Prandelli, 2000a):

- the existence of clear rules of participation, often defined in part by the participants themselves (the capacity to regulate and organize itself), that the members accept when they become registered members;
- spontaneous decision to join based on mechanisms of self-selection designed to ensure that only those who are most willing to share their knowledge and to make a real contribution to the community can participate in the process of distributed learning, since there are tacit sanctions that can be applied if the rules are broken. The result is a high density of potentially 'useful contacts';
- existence of coordinated activities that are centralized and of roles designed to support the ongoing activities of interpersonal communication in order to counterbalance the spontaneity of the contributions and steer these contributions towards the firm's knowledge requirements for its new product development process;
- at least partial codification of explicit knowledge and shared language in order to foster a collective identity that can reinforce the sense of belonging and give rise to socially generated knowledge that is partly tacit since it is rooted in the contexts of individual experiences. At best, a veritable 'electronic paralanguage' is developed within the community. The fact that the observer belongs to the target group is often crucial for this purpose;
- arranging mechanisms of social control by having the users evaluate and cross-check the contributions of each participant in order to check the quality, foster the development of mutually trustworthy resources between members, and eliminate deliberately distorted contributions;
- incentives to participate, namely, mechanisms that can ensure payoffs from the distributed innovation process through tangible recognition – monetary incentives, awards, discounts – and intangible recognition – reputation indexes and the attribution of leadership roles within the community; and
- in the cases of structured processes of distributed innovation, developing rules to redefine intellectual property rights regarding co-created

Table 6.2   The management of a virtual community of consumption as a distributed learning tool: managerial implications

Key questions	Managerial and organizational implications
How much control should be maintained by the firm that starts up the community?	The firm has to help consolidate the rules of participation defined with the users and set the community's rate of development: this attracts individual members and allows them to organize themselves
	It coordinates individual priorities and promotes the creativity of all the participants even if channelled in unforeseen directions
	It helps stabilize individual responsibility and ensure that the solutions proposed are compatible
How can intellectual property rights be guaranteed?	The property rights of the individual have to be maintained as well as the rights of individual innovations developed by specific members when these rights can be apportioned among the community members
	The rights have to be commensurate with the responsibility
What incentives foster long-term involvement?	The firm has to establish tangible and intangible incentives in order to promote the members' contributions
	Mechanisms of social control help make recognition of the individual more objective
How can the community develop?	By maintaining and renewing the balance between continuous innovation and internal cohesion, between excessive creativity and the pursuit of stability
	Tolerating diversity has to co-exist with excessive repetition in order to promote innovation
Can the community continue to remain virtual in the long term?	Over time, virtual interaction often tends to become integrated with some form of physical support
	Firms have to provide different services depending on the intensity of the individual involvement of the members
	In the most advanced cases, the firms can even make available monetary resources to help sustain independent customization of a product

Source: Adapted from Sawhney and Prandelli (2000a).

products since it is often difficult to recognize and appreciate individual contributions.

An interesting example of a virtual community of consumption that can effectively increase the trust of its members over time and systematically contribute to distributed innovation is the case of LEGO. Invented in 1932 by its founder Ole Kirk Christiansen, the traditional LEGO system has, in fact, become a phenomenon capable of promoting the rise of numerous communities of passionate members that have used the Web as a tool to make it easier to share their experiences on a global scale. There are currently over 50 communities of LEGO fans worldwide that have spontaneously decided to aggregate in virtual environments to share their experiences and develop useful innovations such as Ldraw, a 'virtual LEGO' software program, and Moonbase, a new type of multiplayer game. The users are mainly males between the ages of 20 and 40 who spend an average of $2,000 on LEGO products (Antorini, 2005). These are customers who are deeply involved, completely loyal to a brand that the community itself helps develop, and committed to developing aesthetic and functional innovations designed to enrich the products commercialized by the firm. In particular, new designs and instructions to build LEGO are shared by the users of the Brickshelf.com site and in virtual stores the users sell their own projects and products, such as Bricklink.com – the 'Unofficial LEGO Marketplace'. A comparison between the innovations developed by the communities of passionate people and the market trends identified by the American Toy Association clearly shows that virtual communities can shape the future of market demands. Consequently, it is important for firms to interact on a regular basis with these passionate communities that spontaneously aggregate on the Web by making the most of a learning and innovation process that is genuinely distributed and collaborative.

NOTE

1. It is estimated that, on average, a new blog appears every second. The increasing number of weblogs worldwide has reached 27.2 million units (60 times higher than 3 years ago) and, at this rate, the blog universe is expected to double every 5.5 months. In particular, there are 1.2 million daily postings, about 50,000 an hour. (Source: Nextplora, 2006.)

7. Virtual knowledge brokers

7.1 INTRODUCTION

While firms can benefit greatly from engaging directly with customers and communities of customers in virtual environments (VEs), our premise in this book is that direct engagement is not enough. To fully leverage the power of virtual environments, we propose that firms need to combine *direct* channels of customer connection with *mediated* channels that include virtual knowledge brokers (VKBs). These actors manage their own virtual environments and provide these environments as a service to firms. In doing so, they extend a firm's scope of interaction to include knowledge that comes from diverse and previously disconnected sources (Verona et al., 2006).

VKBs are the virtual manifestation of knowledge brokers (KBs) – third parties who connect, recombine and transfer knowledge to companies in order to facilitate innovation (Hargadon and Sutton, 2000). In the physical world, KBs have traditionally taken the form of innovation and design consulting firms (Sutton, 2002; Hargadon, 2003). However, in the virtual world, VKBs take the form of information intermediaries who leverage the unique capabilities of the Internet to absorb valuable market knowledge for innovation. VKBs' activities can be more diverse, their reach is broader, and their influence on the innovation process is qualitatively different. Table 7.1 provides a comparison of operators who use different mechanisms to facilitate innovation.

In physical environments, firms can autonomously innovate or they can involve KBs like the design firms IDEO and Design Continuum to support their innovation activity and obtain specific design solutions. In virtual settings, firms can directly leverage the Internet to engage customers in the innovation process. But they can go beyond direct channels by using VKBs to extend their reach, increase the speed and improve the quality of their innovation activities. VKBs collect dispersed individual and social customer knowledge, and distribute it to firms after organizing and elaborating it to support innovation. They augment the firm's 'network resources' (Gulati, 1999) by enabling the process of distributed innovation (Arora et al., 2002), where the firm becomes the focal node of an interorganizational network of knowledge (Powell et al., 1996; Ahuja, 2000). In this

Table 7.1   A comparison between mechanisms for supporting a firm's innovation process

	VKB	KB	VE
Type of contact	Mediated	Mediated	Direct
Source of knowledge	Industrial and interindustrial	Interindustrial	Industrial
Type of outcome	Knowledge for innovation	Product design	Knowledge for innovation
Role in the process	Invention and innovation	Invention	Invention and innovation
Type of orientation	Network orientation	Client orientation	Firm orientation
Type of interaction	Continuous	Spot	Continuous
Core competence in the brokering cycle	Network access	Absorption and integration	Absorption and implementation
Main limit	Knowledge implementation	Network access	Network access

chapter, after reviewing how virtual environments enable KBs, we discuss how they contribute to the process of innovation. We conclude by providing a taxonomy for VKBs.

7.2   VKBs AND KNOWLEDGE ABSORPTION, INTEGRATION AND IMPLEMENTATION

When knowledge brokers operate in a virtual environment, four specific kinds of Internet-based tools may support *knowledge absorption* from individual customers as well as communities of customers.[1] As we have shown in the previous chapters, first, the Internet makes it possible to directly acquire knowledge through observation of online customer behavior. Marketers can track what customers do on their site (Burke et al., 2001). Second, customers may be asked to participate actively in surveys and pools or online focus groups in order to get their specific feedback. Third, customer preferences for new product concepts can be measured through web-based conjoint analysis tools (Dahan and Hauser, 2002). The Internet also allows customers to self-configure and self-design products, bringing customers directly into the design and development process (Thomke and von Hippel, 2002). Finally, the Internet allows for extending knowledge absorption from individual customers to customers within their own communities, leveraging the social knowledge that develops through spontaneous conversations among them (Kozinets, 1999).

Since in virtual environments any kind of interaction is mediated through electronic interfaces (Hoffman and Novak, 1996), virtual environments have the capability of storing knowledge, enhancing not only absorption but also *knowledge integration*. First, virtual environments empower formal mechanisms of knowledge sharing because information can be transmitted and shared more broadly. Internet-based tools enable knowledge distribution at the intra-company level (through Intranet and groupware systems); the inter-company level (through Extranets and portals); and at the market level (through the Internet and public databases) (Wayland and Cole, 1997). Such formal mechanisms facilitate systematic information access and increase the awareness about available knowledge, thereby making it easier to internalize and recombine the assimilated knowledge. Second, virtual environments also influence informal social integration, intensifying the relational dimension of social interaction through extended connectivity (Kozinets, 1999). Many virtual communities on the Internet are excellent examples of behavior driven by social and community benefits rather than by short-term economic benefits (Rheingold, 1993). Such a context provides good conditions to support effective knowledge creation and exploitation through spontaneous and collective participation. Hence, virtual 'communities of practice' (Brown and Duguid, 1991) can be purposefully developed in order to favor situated (Lave and Wenger, 1991) and distributed learning (Sproull and Kiesler, 1991).

Virtual environments also influence the process of *knowledge implementation*. Any kind of knowledge shared on the Web has to be codified in order to be digitalized (Afuah, 2003). While this makes tacit knowledge more difficult to exchange on the Internet, it does facilitate knowledge memorization, retrieval and recombination (Fahey and Prusak, 1998). An electronic archival and retrieval system facilitate the finding and recombining of modules of knowledge, making it easier for VKBs to internalize and convert knowledge. Data can be received on-demand from a networked system, with no delay or zero latency (Ruefli et al., 2001). By allowing low-cost and real-time access to broad knowledge, virtual environments facilitate the process that combines apparently incongruous sets of information into a new schema that fosters entrepreneurial action and innovation. At the same time, the Internet can make information available to more potential users, thereby increasing the likelihood of finding alternative users (Afuah, 2003). The same piece of knowledge can be leveraged more extensively: the absence of geographical barriers and the opportunities of connectivity across industries enhance the possibilities for *knowledge exploitation*. In virtual environments it is possible not only to identify and get in touch with more users for the same knowledge, but also to allow them to self-signal to directly cooperate in developing a specific application of knowledge. In traditional environments, KBs have to identify new potential users of their knowledge and discover effective ways to reach them; in virtual environments, VKBs can benefit from a reversed process, creating a public repository of their knowledge and promoting contests to stimulate users to find the best applications for their ideas.

Even more radically, VKBs can transform themselves into marketplaces of ideas, where needs for new applications are directly solicited by some users, and other users with specific knowledge can spontaneously cooperate with the VKBs to identify the required applications, as in the case of the Internet-based operator, InnoCentive (Sawhney et al., 2003).

7.3 THE ROLE OF VKBs IN THE MANAGEMENT OF INNOVATION

Having understood how virtual environments amplify the traditional competences of KBs, we now discuss their impact on the management of innovation in contrast to traditional mechanisms. Figure 7.1 provides a description of our conceptual frame.

The goal of a firm that wants to innovate is to produce products and services that are relevant for their served market. In order to do that, firms have always sought to develop a market orientation (Kohli and Jaworski, 1990) because customer input helps to create better new products faster. Other ingredients of the innovation success include the firm's effective R&D and manufacturing routines (Hayes et al., 1988) and the right balance of organizational competences (Verona, 1999).

Internal barriers to continuous innovation – including the people, structures, managerial systems and values – create inertia that prevents adaptation of the innovation system (Leonard-Barton, 1992; Tushman and O'Really, 1997). These barriers can be overcome by outsourcing a part of the creative activity to KBs. These actors provide specific design solutions to firms, because of their interindustrial and interorganizational exposure (Hargadon and Sutton, 1997). Their special vantage point in the knowledge network helps them to bridge the differences between different worlds and enhance creativity by connecting previously separated nodes.

While many of the innovation practices are still rooted in physical environments, the Internet is emerging as an important channel to support a

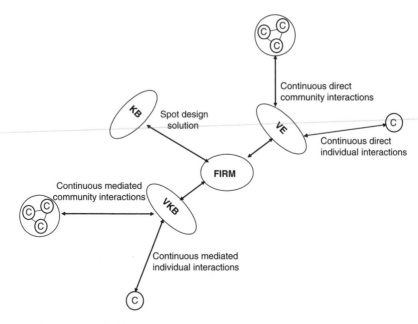

Source: Verona et al. (2006).

Figure 7.1 VKBs as a complementary source of knowledge in managing innovation

firm's innovative capacity. Specifically, while virtual customer environments may be a tremendous source of knowledge for innovation, direct customer engagement is not enough. Direct engagement has in fact a limited network access which may turn into a weakness in the innovation process. Individual firms have limited reach in terms of contexts in which they can enter into a dialogue with customers (Sawhney and Prandelli, 2000b). Customer websites are primarily visited by firms' customers or prospective customers (Nambisan, 2002), but not necessarily by innovative and knowledgeable customers who are invaluable for innovative ideas. Likewise, a firm's website is rarely visited by competitors' customers or by non-adopters. For all of these reasons, VKBs provide an important service to firms in overcoming the structural problem of limited reach between firms and their potential customers by creating single points of contact between firms and millions of potential customers belonging to specific segments (Burke et al., 2001). Thanks to their extended reach, VKBs allow firms to overcome possible myopia arising out of listening only to current customers in narrow contexts.

A further limitation that firms face is their inability to access social customer knowledge. As we have seen, to the extent that consumption phenomena are increasingly influenced by social contexts, knowledge development through peer-to-peer customer interactions becomes critical in defining new product attributes and uses. Customers influence each other considerably in their choice of new products (Rogers, 1995) and contribute to the development of collective meanings (Rheingold, 1993). On the Internet, the opportunity to tap into social customer knowledge is greatly enhanced by virtual customer communities. However, firms need specialized competences to select the right communities to analyze, share their languages, and manage and synthesize customer knowledge emerging through spontaneous interactions and online conversations. Hence, in contexts where social knowledge is important for innovation, firms might find it difficult to collect this distributed knowledge on their own, and therefore may benefit from working with independent actors who can enrich their understanding of customer needs. For example, the apparel company, Diesel, uses third-party websites and communities to obtain crucial social customer knowledge (Verona and Prandelli, 2002).

VKBs also help firms to overcome perceptions of bias that firms may face in soliciting customer input for innovation. Customers often perceive firms as having vested interests, and therefore they may be reluctant to share information openly with the firm. Customers are much more likely to trust an unbiased third party whose sole purpose is to help them by understanding their preferences with regard to products, brands and manufacturers (Hagel and Rayport, 1997). This is why customers rarely tend to speak about their lifestyle and interests on company websites, preferring independent communities where they feel that their knowledge will not be exploited for commercial purposes (Sherry and Kozinets, 2001). Customers are also biased by their experience with the firm, and may not be able to think differently about the firm and its offerings. Rogers (1995) illustrates the role of incompatibility with existing products and behaviors as an important barrier to adoption. Customers are not even always completely aware of their own specific needs and specific solutions that might address their needs. Therefore, they tend to consult autonomous and unbiased third parties early on in the decision process, before they engage with specific firms and products (Maes, 1999). Firms are also informed by their prior experience, which limits their ability to absorb customer knowledge that may not be congruent with them (Christensen, 1997). Therefore, firms that limit their collaboration with existing customers tend to self-confirm their mental models and run the risk of creating innovation that is not relevant for the market at large, and too incremental to sustain competitive advantage (Christensen and Bower, 1996). In order to gain insights that facilitate innovations, firms need to complement the knowledge that they can obtain from their current customers with knowledge from potential customers that the firm may not normally interact with, knows little about, and cannot reach in a credible manner.

The role of VKBs in the management of innovation is also different from traditional KBs. The latter specifically offer new solutions to design problems to firms and therefore contribute primarily to their *inventive* activity. Clients typically hire a KB to design part or all of a product that they would like to manufacture and sell but lack the expertise or staff levels to design. Results range from sketches of product concepts to complete new product design, and the collaboration between the KB and its client tends to last, according to the specific design project, from a few weeks to three years, with an average of about one year (Hargadon and Sutton, 1997). KBs innovate by combining existing technologies originated in several industries in new ways (Hargadon, 1998). Hence, they absorb knowledge from other companies: innovative firms located in different industries are often the source of their ideas, and the main skill of KBs involves finding opportunities by arbitraging knowledge across industry contexts. This recombination and arbitrage allows KBs to serve as a valuable clearinghouse for technological solutions (Hargadon and Sutton, 1997).

VKBs differ from KBs in several key respects. First, they do not offer completely developed design solutions, but provide a service that extends to the entire scope of the innovation activity. Second, they do not leverage solutions and technologies already developed within other companies, but absorb new ideas and knowledge from customers. This requires the creation and ongoing management of two-way interactions with individual customers and virtual communities on a systematic basis. Third, as a consequence, the collaboration between VKBs and firms who work with them is often not limited to an individual project, but can expand over time to support different knowledge needs on an as-needed basis. Clients typically hire a VKB to gather market knowledge in order to enhance either their ability to generate and select new ideas – representing stimuli to incremental but even radical innovation – or their ability to develop, test and refine new products. Hence, by managing knowledge of distant customers, VKBs may be useful in the front- as well as at the back-end stages of the innovation management process. So while KBs tend to have a strong client orientation to serve the needs of a firm looking for a specific design solution, VKBs tend to favor a network orientation, providing knowledge absorbed from customers to different companies, repackaged in different ways, to support different stages of the innovation process.

It is also important to highlight the limitations of VKBs. The processes of absorption and usage, and hence transfer between a firm and a VKB, are all influenced by the nature of knowledge and specifically by the level of knowledge codification. When knowledge is codified, it can also be replicated (Szulanski, 1996).[2] Virtual environments do not allow all types of knowledge to be exchanged. Tacit knowledge is more difficult to exchange over the Internet than explicit knowledge (Afuah, 2003). This does not mean that on the Internet tacit knowledge is not present, since in a virtual community people may exchange ideas and feelings, and also solve problems. It simply means that the lack of codification may limit the ability of a VKB to capture tacit knowledge. Other things being equal, the ability of a VKB to contribute to a firm's innovative activity will be moderated by the level of codification of the knowledge to be absorbed. This is exactly the opposite in the case of a traditional KB. The fact that KBs are rooted in a physical context reduces their ability in network access, but increases their ability to absorb, integrate and implement knowledge. Also, the fact that they work in close proximity with their customers helps them to deliver customized solutions.

7.4   VKBs: TOWARDS A TAXONOMY

While there is a rich academic literature on value co-creation, OSS and communities of creation, the mechanism of VKBs has just started to be discussed in the literature (Verona et al. 2006). Therefore, it is important to analyze this mechanism in more detail. In contrast with other distributed innovation mechanisms, the VKB model is characterized by the presence of a dedicated individual operator (the firm that brokers the knowledge for innovation) which relies on a one-to-one relation with the firm that wants to innovate. Based on primary research across a range of industries, research based on secondary data and document analysis,[3] we have identified four types of VKBs (Prandelli et al., 2006a):

- innovation marketplace;
- customer network operators;
- technology marketplace; and
- community network operators.

As Figure 7.2 shows, some of these VKBs help at the front end of the innovation life cycle, providing insights into the market and customers, while others are more useful at the back end of the process. Another key difference among various types of VKBs is that some of them provide prepackaged knowledge that is not customized to the specific needs of a specific firm, while others work on a customized basis on the specific solutions requested by a client firm. Next, we discuss each of the four types of VKBs in more detail.

Degree of Specialization

Back end   Front end

Transaction	Technology Marketplace e.g. Tech-ex Yet2 Pharmalicensing	Customer Network Operator e.g. ComScore Networks Nielsen BuzzMetrics
Solution	Innovation Marketplace e.g., Innocentive NineSigma	Customer Community Operator e.g., Edmunds Gizmodo

Type of Relationship

Figure 7.2   A taxonomy of VKBs

Technology Marketplace

The technology marketplace operator employs a 'many-to-many' mechanism whose purpose is to connect sellers of technology with potential buyers. The type of knowledge available for sale is the specialized expertise by professionals which has already been pre-codified, typically through patents or licenses that are made public on a dedicated website. The key characteristic of these VKBs is the ability to connect demand and supply on existing relevant problems with innovation for which possible solutions are already available in the broad interindustrial technology market. These operators make money based on a transaction fee for buying a selected technology or intellectual property. Many of these operators also collect fees related to the opportunity to transact. Technology suppliers may be asked for a fee to post their technology on the website; buyers may be asked for a membership fee to get access to a database of technology solutions available for sale. While most technology marketplaces are interindustrial, these VKBs tend to focus on industries that rely heavily on patents (for example, chemical, biotech and pharmaceuticals). To study this type of VKB in more detail, we describe two such entities – Yet2.com and TechEx.

Yet2.com was founded in 1999, in Cambridge, Massachusetts, and in a short period of time it has become the biggest worldwide market for patents. Specifically, it has extensive experience in matching demand and supply for intellectual property assets: from patents to complete packages of technology and know-how. The purpose is to allow all parties to maximize the return on their investments. Whether the users are working with a team of their licensing experts or using the virtual technology marketplace, Yet2.com offers companies and individuals the tools and expertise to acquire, sell, license and leverage valuable intellectual assets. In 2002, Yet2.com was bought by Schiper Plc, a British company leading in patent and product licensing across Europe. With over 100,000 users in June 2007, Yet2.com represents more than 30 categories, including chemicals, new materials, electronics and consumer goods. As a technology marketplace, the company is a traditional many-to-many operator, where seekers of specific technologies may find sellers of patents. Sellers can remain anonymous until they have identified a buyer and they can set restrictions, exercise listings at any time, and accept only the introductions they consider adequate. Potential buyers can be supported in their search for a specific technology by services such as the 'Free patent search' which allow users to save, manage and organize their patent search, and the 'Consult with an expert' which provides professional consulting and expert witness services from over 11,000 subject matter experts covering 30,000 areas of science, engineering, regulation and business. Seekers of specific technologies can remain anonymous, but they have to provide some information such as company type, annual revenue, years in business and geographic area of their activity. The TechNeed Challenge periodically highlights TechNeeds that individuals and their organization may be able to meet. A description of the required technology is provided, together with a desired timeframe, the field of use, intended application and the desired outcome. Among the customers that sponsor and use the website are large companies such as 3M, Honeywell, the Boeing Company, the Dow Chemical Company, DuPont, P&G and other international companies such as Toyota Motors and Bayer.

TechEx has built a network of research and licensing professionals in the biomedical industry, providing a virtual marketplace for buying and selling biomedical technologies in five main areas: agriculture, chemicals, diagnostics, genomics and medical equipment. Founded at Yale University at the end of the 1990s and acquired by UTEK Corporation in May 2002, TechEx is used by thousands of technology transfer and research professionals to efficiently exchange licensing opportunities and innovations available for partnering. It is considered a premier source for emerging technologies in the biomedical field. New discoveries from corporate, government and academic laboratories are listed at Techex.com every day. These technologies are immediately compared against the interests of the world's leading biotechnology development organizations to ensure the fastest communication of biomedical breakthroughs. TechEx is a members-only system and is restricted to approved users.

There are three types of participants: licensing professionals from research institutions; corporate licensing professionals capable of bringing early-stage inventions to market or otherwise providing significant value-added development; and venture capitalists capable of providing financial assistance to commercialization efforts. At the buyer end, corporate licensing professionals and venture capitalists establish a confidential and secure interest profile describing licensing opportunities of interest to them. They can specify the specific applications or pathologies they are interested in, define the development stage (from discovery to Phase II), set geographical limitations, and define technological sources (for example, research centers or corporations only). At the seller end, research institutions and corporations with technologies to license provide non-confidential descriptions of their technologies. They have to specify the industry where these technologies are applicable, the licensing conditions, and the type of partnership they are interested in. TechEx matches opportunities with interests and sends complete information to all parties. TechEx features thousands of inventions from over 600 corporations and 340 research institutions. A division of UTEK – Pax Technology Transfer Ltd – operates in Europe to assist local clients. Another ad hoc organizational unit has been created to serve the Asian market. TechEx has two main revenue sources: an annual fee ($2,500) and a fee per listing ($250). As an option, users can also pay a predefined amount of money to gain unlimited access to the TechEx website and its services. There are no commissions on completed transactions and non-profit institutions do not have to pay a fee per listing. Universities can also create 'Gateway' websites for free to sell their own technologies and buy new ones. For instance, Harvard University has set up the Harvard Biomedical Community Technology Gateway to aggregate and provide visibility to all the research activities run by Harvard in the biomedical field.

Innovation Marketplace

An innovation marketplace is also a many-to-many operator. In this case, the innovations are typically intellectual property – a discovery, patent or kind of know-how. The main difference between these VKBs and the technology marketplace is that the innovation marketplace works on a customized basis to provide ad hoc transactions for specific customers. In so doing, it goes beyond offering a prepackaged technology or patent by providing solutions on request and consulting services related to innovation.

To understand how innovation marketplace operators function, consider the InnoCentive case we have already described in Chapter 4. InnoCentive's approach is very different from the way contract research is typically outsourced. Its process has four steps. First, scientists review the problems posted by companies in need of solutions; the details of each problem include a molecular structure, problem specifications, the cash incentive, and the deadline for submission of proposed solutions. Next, if scientists wish to participate in the competition, they register on the site as potential problem solvers. In the third step, they choose a specific problem to work on, sign the agreement that transfers ownership of the resulting intellectual property to the company, and are allocated a 'project room' where they can deploy their work, either as individuals or as members of a team. The project room is a virtual space on the site that allows scientists to post submissions, store documents, and conduct conversations with the seeker company in order to get clarifications or further details about the challenge. Eventually, they can upload a proposed solution in their project room. In the final step, InnoCentive reviews all the proposed solutions, determines the best one that can be reproduced in a laboratory, and awards a cash prize to the scientist or team that came up with the winning solution.

For seeker companies, InnoCentive is a cost-effective, convenient and speedy mechanism for tapping into scientific knowledge distributed across the globe. It allows them to expand their R&D capacity flexibly without adding to employee costs. Since all payments are contingent upon satisfactory solutions, companies incur no additional expenses as more and more solvers take on a specific problem. Further, because scientists from diverse disciplines and locations can address the innovation challenges, problems that were deemed unsolvable have been conquered by scientists from very different disciplines who have taken unconventional approaches to solving problems from outside their fields. For potential problem solvers, InnoCentive provides an easy and quick way to find challenging problems that match their experience and expertise, and offers the promise of a financial reward.

By June 2007, more than 120,000 scientists from 175 countries had registered on InnoCentive's website, and more than half of that number came from outside the United States. In the first half of 2007, over 30 awards had been announced ranging from $2,000 to $100,000, and several dozen more were in the pipeline. Scientists who participate include retired researchers, university professors, researchers working for independent clinical research organizations, and even scientists working for non-competing pharmaceutical firms. Although the cash payments are often modest by US standards, they are significant for scientists from developing countries. The satisfaction of solving a difficult problem also seems to motivate many scientists to participate in InnoCentive challenges. Innovation marketplace operators such as InnoCentive blend the benefits of the distributed mechanism that are central to the success of the open-source approach to innovation with those that come from having a sponsor organization that coordinates the marketplace, sets the ground rules, gains trust and creates incentives for participation. The innovation marketplace operator maintains the balance between structure and chaos that is so important in managing distributed innovation.

Customer Network Operators

While technology and innovation marketplaces work on the back end of the innovation process, the other two VKBs work at its front end with the specific objective of importing the voice of the customer to facilitate early stages of the innovation process. Customer network operators are like online versions of market research vendors that operate customer panels. They support innovation by recruiting and maintaining networks of customers and providing companies access to specific customer segments for the purpose of soliciting feedback. Customer network operators are most useful in the stages of concept testing or test marketing, when firms want to know how customers will react to new product concepts or new products. Firms interact with customers through surveys or by monitoring purchase behavior, so the knowledge they obtain is explicit rather than tacit. In other words, they can use the VKB to find out what customers 'know they know' and what they actually purchase, but not what they know but cannot express directly or what they do without being fully aware of their behavior.

An example of a customer network operator is the online market research company comScore Networks, which has recruited a global sample of more than 1.5 million panelists who have agreed to have their Internet behavior confidentially and anonymously monitored. The company uses this large panel to provide information to companies about their customers, their competitors' customers, or prospective customers; it tracks what people buy, how often, from which sites, and how they respond to online advertising and marketing offers. comScore aggregates the panelists' online buying information and combines it with data about their offline buying behavior (gleaned from such sources as retail-store scanners and credit card databases) to create a 'customer knowledge platform' – a 360-degree view of the surfing and buying behavior of customers over the entire Internet. In addition to general customer-buying behavior, comScore offers a 'private network service' to companies that want to understand and interact with specific customer segments. To set up a private network, comScore recruits a panel of customers in accordance with the client's needs and then monitors their Internet activities. Companies can use private networks to test alternative new product concepts, marketing offers and marketing communications with a select group of customers located within a 'walled garden'. The company also allows its private network clients to conduct surveys so that they can collect preference and perceptual data in addition to behavioral data.

Customer Community Operators

While customer network operators help companies to import knowledge from individual customers, they cannot help with knowledge that is generated through interactions *among* customers. The customer community operator is a VKB that specializes in connecting firms with customers who form a community based on common interests. Community operators commonly begin life as Infomediaries, creating communities in order to facilitate transactions. They then evolve into a VKB role. They are particularly useful at the ideation stage in the innovation process, when companies are trying to understand customer lifestyles, motivations and unmet needs. They are also valuable at the product design stage, when product designers and managers need to communicate and collaborate with customers to optimize the designs. Community operators can also help companies to identify and profile influencers and opinion leaders within a customer population, to shape the opinions of early adopters, and to accelerate the diffusion of new products through word of mouth or 'word of mouse'.

An example of a community operator is Edmunds (www.edmunds.com), an Infomediary that empowers automotive customers to make better buying and ownership decisions by providing detailed and unbiased information for automobile buyers. Edmunds focuses on editorial content and community management, and generates revenues by referring qualified leads to marketing partners that include auto dealers, manufacturers, finance and insurance companies. More recently, Edmunds has begun to act as a VKB. It realized that its community named Town Hall could actually be a valuable resource for its automobile original equipment manufacturer (OEM) partners. It now allows automobile OEM executives to host discussions as guests or to answer questions posed by customers. OEM product managers can even create their own sub-communities about, for example, a new model that they may be bringing to market in the future. Some automotive companies have gone further, creating private communities for which they pay Edmunds a monthly fee to host and run their part of the site. For instance, Edmunds's partners, such as Subaru, have begun to make use of its million-strong customer community to obtain specific feedback from a diverse group of customers regarding their products. This feedback is analyzed and repackaged by Edmunds to suit Subaru's specific knowledge needs and to support its new product development activities. By partnering with Edmunds, Subaru can maximize the quality of customer contributions and filter out less-insightful conversations. When Edmunds hosts live chat events, it is able to engage more than 200 participants per session, who act as a clinical group, providing comments, advice about products, and product experiences to a product manager, who can intervene to appropriately stimulate their knowledge sharing. Beyond operating ad hoc virtual communities, Edmunds has also created an offering called Edmunds Information Solutions for automotive manufacturers, which provides competitive intelligence, consideration sets, customer preferences and buying behavior to support the new product development and product marketing processes for automotive OEMs. In this way Edmunds helps OEMs to connect with customers who are more committed, active and informed than those who visit websites run by individual manufacturers.

In a similar way, but in a different industry, the community operator Liquid Generation (www.liquidgeneration.com) provides information useful to firms interested in better understanding teenagers who belong to the so-called 'Generation Y', a segment whose economic importance is increasing. When the company was founded in August 2000, it planned to create a portal and generate revenue through advertising and selling merchandise. However, the firm soon realized that the real opportunities lay in addressing a problem faced by every firm that seeks to market to teenagers: understanding the fickle needs of this population, and motivating hard-to-reach teenagers to provide information about their needs and preferences. The website functions as an entertainment site that hires young people who understand the culture and can interact effectively with the target demographic that the company wants to involve in deep conversations. This content is analyzed and interpreted by Liquid Generation to answer its clients' needs of specific feedback and ideas related to individual products. For instance, one of the firm's clients – a company that makes sweaters – wanted to survey the age group about a new product and its most appropriate attributes. Liquid Generation incorporated the survey questions in a funny online presentation, leveraged its relationships with 3.5 million unique visitors a month, and in about 36 hours was able to provide relevant customer input to its client.

In conclusion, the various types of VKBs can help firms to overcome the limitations that they face in directly engaging with customers in co-creation. They help firms to extend their reach, and to engage with customers without the perception of bias, in contexts that they would find it difficult to do on their own. By tapping into VKBs, firms can harness the power of mediated innovation to complement their direct innovation efforts. Sometimes, communities themselves become creators of innovation, and the role of the firm is no longer that of a dominant sponsor. This phenomenon of community-based innovation, or open-source systems (OSS) is the focus of our attention in the next chapter.

NOTES

1. See Verona et al. (2006) for a complete review.
2. Tacit knowledge does not necessarily mean that it is knowledge that cannot be codified. Individuals and firms can undertake processes of socialization and externalization that may help to codify tacit knowledge (Nonaka and Takeuchi, 1995). Still, some knowledge is unlikely ever to be explicated because it may be embedded in individual or organization cognition and abilities (Leonard and Sensiper, 1998). In this sense, the quantity and quality that may be transmitted depends very much on the level of knowledge codification: codes help transmission, and with low codifiability knowledge transfer is weak.
3. There is little academic literature on the organizational experience of firms that act as VKBs. Hence, we adopt an exploratory approach to derive patterns and implications. We have followed the logic of grounded theory (Glaser and Strauss, 1967), by employing a multiple case-study methodology (Eisenhardt, 1989; Miles and Huberman, 1994). In the tradition of other qualitative approaches used in business research, we rely on a small number of highly visible examples of the object of our inquiry to develop our insights (Pettigrew, 1990). The companies we selected are intensively leveraging the Internet to engage actors for third parties' innovation purposes. Our case studies were based upon a series of in-depth interviews with senior managers. The interviewees within each firm were chosen on the basis of their specialized knowledge and experience, following a key informant approach (Philipps, 1981; Kumar et al., 1993). In-depth interviews were conducted during 2003 and early 2004. The approach was nondirective, based on individual semi-structured interviews (McCracken, 1990) that are flexible, but also controlled (Burgess, 1982). An open-question frame helped us in categorizing the key themes. The analysis also included a detailed archival and Internet data collection based on financial statements, internal documents and industry publications.

8. Open-source systems

8.1 INTRODUCTION

This chapter is devoted to the most open and etherarchical development model to support distributed innovation: open-source systems (OSS). As mentioned in Chapter 5, OSS are an outgrowth of virtual communities. They are run by and for the users to provide themselves with mutual technical assistance (Constant et al., 1996) and create new products or services (Kogut and Metiu, 2001; von Hippel, 2001). More specifically, these systems can be described as Internet-based communities. The members are typically developers who group together spontaneously to develop software for their own use or for the firms they belong to. For some time now, OSS have become an important cultural and economic phenomenon (von Krogh, 2003) and now represent a real innovation model, the so-called 'Private–Collective Innovation Model', which reconciles the diametrically opposite features of the *Private Investment Model*, based on a monopoly control of knowledge for innovation, and the *Collective Action Model*, which makes knowledge for innovation a public good that belongs to the public domain and cannot be withheld from its use (von Hippel and von Krogh, 2003).

According to Giuri et al. (2007), up to now, most theoretical studies on OSS have focused attention on what motivates participants to share their knowledge, the social norms and collaborative methods the developers agree to adopt, and the implications for business and society (for example, von Hippel, 2001; Lerner and Tirole, 2002). Empirical studies have studied the performances of OSS compared to traditional software development models in terms of quality, response time to problems the user encounters, stability and security (for example, Wheeler, 2002).

In this chapter, we investigate the specific nature and potential of OSS as a tool for distributed innovation. We begin with a brief overview of how OSS first developed and became established in order to understand how they are used in distributed innovation. Next, we underline the most relevant underlying principles to profitably manage OSS, focusing mainly on the different types of incentives that promote and support the widest and most systematic participation possible. We also discuss why firms adopt the open-source model to support activities related to NPD and the implications for the management of distributed innovation processes.

8.2   OSS CHARACTERISTICS

The first forms of OSS developed just like the Internet. In 1969, the US Department of Defense created ARPAnet, the first high-speed computer network diffused on a global scale. At that time, it was natural for software developers – from universities, government agencies or corporate laboratories – to use this system to exchange their program codes and other information on a large scale easily and cheaply. As pointed out in Chapter 5, this culture of sharing – also called 'hacker culture' (Levy, 1984) – was particularly widespread among a group of programmers who worked at MIT's Laboratory of Artificial Intelligence. Richard Stallman, who was part of the group, established the Free Software Foundation in 1985 in order to create a legal mechanism for the unrestricted free exchange of software.

The idea of creating software that is freely available was not very successful and was regarded with suspicion by an industry that feared the possible viral effects of the General Public License (GPL) developed by Stallman, which transformed the traditional term of 'copyright' into 'copyleft'. Although the GPL was based on laws that protect copyright, it overturned them to obtain the opposite effect: instead of a way to privatize software, copyleft licenses make software freely available so that anyone could use, copy, modify and distribute adapted versions but without authorizing any restriction. In this way, the basic freedoms, referred to as 'free software', were guaranteed to anyone who possessed a copy, and became an inalienable right. Although firms were initially rather suspicious of this new way of developing innovation, they changed their mind when the label was changed from 'free' to 'open' software in 1998 (Perens, 1999). The open-source software continues to use the same forms of licenses developed by the Free Software Movement. However, OSS distances itself from the Movement from a philosophical standpoint and emphasizes the practical benefits of the licenses rather than emphasizing the importance, from an ethical standpoint, of ensuring users the freedoms introduced by free software. The term 'open source' is now used by firms as well as universities to underline the principle of engaging all the available, distributed competences to participate in a joint process of NPD. This is the essence of OSS, consolidated even more by the recent advances in the Internet, networking technologies, and the ready-made infrastructure support available on the Web (von Hippel, 2005).

More specifically, what ensures the possibility of jointly developing software is the nature of public goods that are characterized by nonrivalry in their consumption, which is typical of software programs. Since they are intangible goods they can be duplicated easily and diffused cheaply (Vicari, 2001), while the nonrivalry in the consumption implies that the use of the product by some users does not reduce the consumption by others (Olson, 1967). The development of a program usually starts by identifying a need not completely satisfied by the available offer. The starting point can be represented by an existing code that needs to be improved or expanded, or a code developed by one individual that requires the collaboration of other users to develop it (Raymond, 1999). If some individuals find this code useful, they can join the project by making their knowledge available, fixing possible bugs or other software problems rather than making suggestions, giving ideas or referring to projects that already exist or are being developed. Moreover, those who join the common project should share the same values based on principles of reciprocity and meritocracy, and adopt only informal development methods and management systems according to the rationale of a 'gift economy'[1] rather than a market economy (for example, Di Bona et al., 1999).

The collaboration of users that group together spontaneously leads to creative chaos. Raymond (2001) effectively represents this chaos by using the 'bazaar' as a metaphor for the babel of voices expressing different opinions, with each person having something to contribute. This is how Linux developed. It juxtaposed the traditional process of developing a program, which is similar to building a cathedral where a few people or small groups work behind closed doors according to a precise hierarchical order. In this case, possible bugs or programming errors need to be carefully worked out by experts and recurrent checks made, with long intervals between one 'release' and another. Instead, according to the approach represented by the bazaar, the 'bugs' are considered marginal, or tend to rapidly become so, if they come to the attention of thousands of co-developers that regularly test each new software version, giving rise to a parallel debugging. Although, theoretically, efficiency is lost due to some duplication of work, this is offset by a 'release early and often' policy (Torvalds and Diamond, 2001) since problem solutions found by the users are rapidly diffused. Therefore, at the system level, these users adopt the best testing methods in the sector (Vixie, 1999) and produce a higher-quality output in a considerably shorter period of time than traditional development processes.[2]

However, as the number of participants grows, the situation becomes more complex and new needs tend to emerge. This often leads to the formation of different interested groups that develop spontaneously within the same community, each working on a sub-problem while simultaneously developing a solution that is functional and compatible with those developed by the other sub-set of groups. It is this phenomenon that has contributed to the success of modular programs: each module is written in the same programming language and the code includes the same variables common to all the other modules and which derive from the original functional structure that was developed. The modular system reduces the interdependence of the different files of the same program and promotes the division of labor, thus reducing the costs of coordinating the groups involved (Garud et al., 2002). This ensures homogeneity, and within the same community, different sub-sets of individuals are empowered to work around specific sub-sets of problems in order to exploit the professional capabilities of the developers. Whether these numerous sub-sets of work emerge clearly depends on the complexity of the project that has to be developed.

In any case, in order to ensure that individual contributions are directed towards a specific target with respect to the original objectives, there has to be a credible coordinator. According to Lerner and Tirole (2002), the coordinator has to have a clear vision, divide the project into modules, and attract other developers. The rationale is to motivate these developers by delegating them as much work as possible without ever losing sight of the original task in order to prevent 'code forking', a counterproductive bifurcation of the project. In order to prevent this, the community can adopt two specific strategies: first, 'flaming', that is, publicly condemning the 'guilty' party by means of a smear campaign; second, 'shunning', that is, isolating the highjacker by forbidding him/her to participate in cooperative software development since he/she has violated social norms sanctioned by the community itself.

As shown in Table 8.1, there are important differences between proprietary and open-source software. In the development of proprietary software, the value system is focused on profit, the process is *organization-centric*, personnel are divided according to precise rules, decentralization is limited, the information flow is restricted by internal communication channels, and leadership is based on experience and seniority. In the development of open software, voluntary work and meritocracy prevail, the process is *project-centric*, resources are self-selected, decentralization is extensive, the information flow in the relational network is free, and leadership is based on the trust and consensus of the reference community (Iannacci, 2002).

If we look more closely at the specific features of the two types of software, we see that they differ in three fundamental ways. First, the relationship between the producer and the software users is different: while in the case of commercial software there is a precise separation between those who produce the program and those who use it, in the case of open software the interaction between producers and users is more intense and more frequent and includes the entire community. Second, while the software house usually limits access to the source code – and possible variations – only to the firm's collaborators or third parties through a contractual agreement, in OSS everyone has access to the source code, however contrary to

Table 8.1 Development models of proprietary and open software: a comparative analysis

	Proprietary software	Open software
Value system	Centered on profits: limited strategies and activities to improve process and product quality	Voluntarism, freedom and meritocracy: the outcome of the development process is usually of high quality
Focus	Organization-centric	Project-centric
Selection of resources	Selecting, hiring and training of personnel; allocation to projects according to precise rules	Self-selection of the resources on the basis of the attractiveness of the projects
Decentralization	Limited; top-down approach Slow innovation and lower innovation content of product	Extensive; bottom-up approach Search for alternatives and rapid innovation
Information flow	Restricted by internal communication channels; high control costs	Free within the network of relationships activated; limited coordination costs
Leadership	Based on experience and service seniority; decision-making process concentrated in the hands of a few people	Meritocracy; leadership based on trust and consensus; decision-making power resides in the community; more impartial decisions

Source: Adapted from Iannucci (2002).

what the GPL originally stated, restrictions can be applied to the use and exchange of software in order to guarantee the integrity of the original code and maximize access to the modified program (for example, Meyer and Lopez, 1995). Finally, there are substantial differences regarding the license. Open-source software is protected by a license that is not standard: the authors are free to prescribe a number of conditions that the users have to comply with in order to download the program. These conditions usually refer to a set of licenses approved by the Open Source Initiative that differ in four ways from proprietary software:

- open software can be combined and supplemented with commercial software;
- the modifications can be kept private and not given back to the author;
- the software can be relicensed by anyone; and

- the software contains special privileges regarding modifications for those holding the original copyright.

Unlike commercial software licenses, in which intellectual property rights protect the author's right to the profits gained from the innovation, the norms regarding open software have been conceived to guarantee the right against the appropriation by future users so that the contributions of the individual remain the property of the community itself. O'Mahony (2003) points out that it is important for developers who participate in OSS projects to ensure that their contributions remain an integral part of the common project. For this purpose, he identifies seven basic strategies to prevent proprietary appropriation:

- adopt software licenses that limit proprietary appropriation by including measures designed to prevent the distribution of public goods;
- promote compliance with licenses by means of normative and legal sanctions;
- set up associations, legal bodies and non-profit foundations capable of preserving intellectual property rights and protecting voluntary contributions from the risk of appropriation;
- transfer individual property rights to a foundation since these rights are better defined and easier to protect if held by a single legal body,[3]
- trademark the brands and logos designed to represent their work;
- transfer these trademarks to the foundations or non-profit bodies that support the project;[4] and
- actively protect the software's brand, especially if programs are repackaged and distributed by the firms.

A comparison of the different means of developing and protecting open and proprietary software has to be supplemented by considering the performance of each. If we consider fixing bugs as a proxy of quality, it has been shown that the results obtained by open software are much greater. This is due to the great number of the external contributions (von Hippel, 2001) and to the fact that external programmers can directly solve problems (Hecker, 1999). The rate of external contributions, the diversification and level of experience of the competences, as well as the variety of the target users can also influence project performance (Giuri et al., 2007). In particular, the larger the community of potential users – for example, final consumers, developers and system administrators – the greater the potential contribution of the community can be to product development.

8.3 MANAGERIAL AND ORGANIZATIONAL IMPLICATIONS FOR DISTRIBUTED INNOVATION

The critical tools and infrastructures needed to support the participants engaged in an open software project are designed to facilitate interaction and include, first of all, e-mail lists created for specialized objectives. Usually, ad hoc lists are created so users can report software problems. There is also a list dedicated to the developers where they can share information about how to further develop the program and the functions that need to be added. These lists are available to all the contributors and the content is placed in public archives so that anyone can have free access to the opinions regarding a specific topic arranged in chronological order. Programmers can also access a common programming language that is not necessarily defined univocally for every single project but is often freely available on the Web. There is also software that can test and check the compatibility of new versions of the code so that new contributions do not cause the original code to malfunction. Should this occur, these tools can immediately re-establish the original code. Therefore, programmers are encouraged to use a 'try it and see' approach in order to reduce risks in experimentation (von Hippel, 2005).

The appropriate use of this kind of tool allows OSS to be an effective alternative to the traditional use of innovation processes that von Hippel and von Krogh (2003) trace back to the Private Investment Model and the Collective Action Model. The first model assumes that the innovation is supported by private investment and that the return on investment can be appropriated (Demsetz, 1967). In other words, the Private Investment Model generates profits for the innovator through the use of private goods and investment that are protected by laws regarding intellectual property mechanisms such as patents and copyrights. The monopoly control of knowledge tries to prevent any kind of 'spillover' and the profits from such spillover represent a loss to society since the knowledge is no longer freely available. Society accepts this social loss in order to increase the incentives of the innovators that invest in the creation of new knowledge.

The Collective Action Model applies to the provision of public goods defined by their nonexcludability and nonrivalry (Olson, 1967). The fulcrum of this model is the collaboration between innovators. The basic presumption is that whoever contributes to the development of the output relinquishes control of the knowledge generated for a specific project, and transforms it into a public good that is freely offered for the benefit of society. Given this premise, it is clear that problems can arise regarding how to motivate the participants. In this connection, it is fundamental to develop some form of ad hoc incentives that can be temporary or based on reputation as commonly occurs when scientific knowledge is produced.

OSS represents an effective compromise between these two extremes, giving rise to what von Hippel and von Krogh (2003) define as the 'Private–Collective Model'. According to this model, those who collaborate in an open software project use their own resources and invest them to develop a new program, but relinquish their intellectual property rights in order to make the program available to everyone as if it were a public good. Therefore, what is created is a model of innovation development that can offer society the best of both worlds: funds and private contributions generate new knowledge that anyone can freely access and use.

In particular, the Private–Collective Model differs from the Private Investment Model in two ways:

- the software innovators use the software and do not produce it; and
- the innovators freely reveal the source code of the software they have developed at their own expense.

There are two reasons why manufacturers have traditionally been considered the usual developers of new products. First, because their financial capacity is usually higher than for users since manufacturers can sell their output across the entire market. On the contrary users obtain financial benefits from their innovations only if they use them themselves. If they decided to diffuse their output to others they would have to adopt measures protecting intellectual property rights through license agreements. Second, manufacturers have a well-organized 'supply chain', and, by exploiting the positive effects of economies of scale and learning, they can benefit from diffusing innovation as much as possible. In fact, innovators can obtain benefits by amply sharing the software, exploiting network effects, and by selling complementary goods and services when there is low rivalry with potential users. This possibility is anything but sporadic considering that most participants in OSS are students. Because of these phenomena, in open-source software projects, the costs related to the loss of intellectual property rights as well as diffusion are low. Consequently, even modest incentives can be enough to motivate potential participants (Lerner and Tirole, 2002).

The Private–Collective Model also differs from the Collective Action Model which represents a response to the failure of the market. On the basis of the literature on collective action, in order for such a model to work, it is important to recruit and motivate the participants so that they will take an interest and make contributions instead of behaving like 'free riders', and also to point out the benefits of a long-term cooperative relationship. To this end, ad hoc incentives must also be provided. Once again,

OSS do not seem to follow any of these guidelines. In fact, preference is given to mechanisms of self-selection, and in general, specific measures to encourage active participation, instead of free riding, are not implemented. According to von Hippel and von Krogh (2003), this is possible because, in open-source software development projects, the private benefits obtained by the person actively involved in the project are much greater than those obtained by free riders. In other words, contributions made to OSS projects are not assimilated to public goods but continue to maintain private elements even after the contributions are made freely accessible.

In this way, the Private–Collective Model comes close to closing the irreconcilable gap between the Private Investment Model and the Collective Action Model by eliminating two key assumptions:

- the assumption of the first model that claims that open access to innovations developed with private resources necessarily represents a profit loss for innovators and consequently will not be undertaken voluntarily. In fact, under specific conditions – for example, by diffusing the innovation in order to benefit from network effects – making the innovation available without restrictions can result in a net gain in terms of private profit; and
- the conviction of the second model that claims that a free rider can obtain the same benefits as those obtained by a contributor to the development of a completely public good can enjoy. On the contrary, in accordance with the Private–Collective Model, contributors to the development of a public good can enjoy benefits that are intrinsic and exclusive and can boast of incentives connected to learning, the reputation acquired, and the sense of control over the work carried out.

Based on these premises, an open-source project can therefore be activated by anyone who has the appropriate knowledge and motivation. However, the success of the project depends on the capacity to take up the challenges successfully (von Krogh, 2003). One challenge is to succeed in getting the best programmers to participate. In fact, in some cases, these programmers even prefer working on open-source projects rather than on commercial initiatives. In fact, it is often difficult to understand in advance the features that can best satisfy the demand. Even the users find it difficult to completely express their needs (von Hippel, 1998). This makes firms develop standard software packages that can satisfy the largest possible public in order to spread the high development and marketing costs, knowing, however, that the market launch of the product might not be successful. It is this risk that can contribute to making developers participate in an open-source project where they can work on developing a program that can really satisfy their technical and practical requirements (Raymond, 1999). More generally, the best programmers tend to prefer the biggest and most successful projects that allow them to confront a wider public and thus considerably augment their reputation (Lerner and Tirole, 2002; Dalle and David, 2003).

A second important challenge is how to organize support for the innovation process. The *for-profit* programming firms often try to cut development costs and control the quality of the output by monitoring the development process itself (Cusumano, 1992). In order to ensure a satisfactory return on the innovation investment, they try to hire the most talented people and bind them to the firm through contracts and measures to minimize any kind of opportunistic behavior (Austin, 2001). Moreover, in order to prevent the transfer of information or important technologies to competitors they often encourage specialization and apportion the work among the developers so that nobody has a complete picture of the entire project. On the contrary, those working on OSS projects participate voluntarily and have no formal contract. The project leader cannot make the participants prolong or increase the efforts they put into the project. Moreover, the participants also come to value the sense of ownership and control over their work (Lakhani and von Hippel, 2003) without even attempting to minimize the risks of free riding (Moon and Sproull, 2000). Although no formal mechanisms are required to regulate the division of labor, there is heavy emphasis on transparency: everyone has access to complete e-mailing lists and software source code. As often stressed, the objective is to promote the largest possible diffusion of the program in order to augment the reputation of the developers and diffuse the products they have developed.

Although a firm's personnel office can recruit the best collaborators, there are no formal recruiting mechanisms to hire collaborators for an open-source project. This could lead to hiring less-qualified collaborators and jeopardize the overall quality of the software. In fact, it has been demonstrated that the developer community fully conforms to the principles of meritocracy, and technical expertise and experience are the only variables that influence the impact that each participant has on the final definition of the program. According to a research study carried out by von Krogh et al. (2003) on a peer-to-peer software development project called Freenet, only 30 per cent of the participants had the right to include the code in the official version of the software. In order to be admitted to this restricted developer community, they had to demonstrate a level of technological competence much higher than the other participants. OSS projects also tend to favor a process of self-organization of the resources.

Participants are not assigned tasks based on a predefined work project but according to their personal interests and a self-selection mechanism (Kogut and Metiu, 2001; Koch and Schneider, 2002). The merit of this method is that the groups form spontaneously and the competence is extremely high. However, the key risk of this self-organization approach is that, in the absence of centralized coordination of activities, some fundamental program modules may never be developed (Sawhney and Prandelli, 2000a). In order to eliminate this risk, some OSS projects have developed a kind of division of labor between a small group of core developers who develop the source code, and a larger number of peripheral programmers who suggest ways to improve the quality of the final output. This is exemplified by Apache, which has 15 project organizers dedicated to defining the new functionality of the base code, 250 core developers and over 3,000 users that belong to the enlarged community and help identify possible bugs (Mockus et al., 2000).

OSS can provide important insights into the effective organization and management of distributed innovation processes (Chesbrough, 2003). The lesson OSS teaches resides in the value of the specialization through self-selection and the importance of reputation through *peer-to-peer* mechanisms that ensure the quality of the final output (von Krogh, 2003). As pointed out in Chapter 6, these two principles are also fundamental requisites in transforming virtual communities into learning tools. At this point, the key problem is finding the right portfolio of incentives to motivate the best resources to participate in the increasingly open innovation processes.

In particular, economic theory, with the contribution of sociology, has identified various mechanisms that can act as incentives to motivate participation and knowledge sharing within the community environment. In particular, in their extensive review of the literature, Feller and Fitzgerald (2002) have identified three principal areas of incentives corresponding to different *payoffs* that can motivate users to participate in a development community, specifically, an OSS development project (Table 8.2).

The first category refers to incentives of an economic nature. It includes financial compensation, often adopted by firms that use part of their labor force in such situations. The low opportunity costs, namely, the possibility of using specific software freely or at a much lower cost than proprietary software, provide the chance to enhance peer reputation. Dalle and David (2003) include reputation-based financial incentives among the economic incentives, since once a reputation is acquired in an environment considered important by the software house, this can lead to career advancement and a higher salary. The future benefits in terms of career, according to

Table 8.2   Incentives to motivate participation and relevant literature

Area of motivation	Type of incentive	Relevant literature
Economic	Monetary compensation	Feller and Fitzgerald (2002); Lerner and Tirole (2002)
	Reduced cost opportunity	Kollock (1999); Bonaccorsi and Rossi (2003); Lakhani and von Hippel (2003)
	Peer-to-peer reputation	Bezroukov (1999); Dalle and David (2003)
	Future career benefits	Lerner and Tirole (2002)
Social	Enjoyment	Green (2000); Torvalds and Diamond (2001)
	Altruism	Mauss (1959); Raymond (1999); Bergquiest and Ljungberg (2001)
	Sense of belonging to the community	David and Pfaff (1998); Raymond (2001)
	The campaign 'to fight' against proprietary software	Stallman (1984)
Technological	Learning	Lakhani and von Hippel (2003)
	Contributions and feedback from community	Raymond (2001); Bonaccorsi and Rossi (2003)
	Access to a new technology	David and Pfaff (1998); Pavlicek (1999); von Hippel and von Krogh (2003)
	Solving a personal problem	Green (2000); Feller and Fitzgerald (2002); Franke and von Hippel (2003)

Source: Adapted from Feller and Fitzgerald (2002).

a principle analogous to the previous one, are based on the assumption that participation can improve IT-related programming skills and organizational competence.

The second category of incentives regards the social dimension, including the benefits related to the enjoyment related to programming and altruism. According to the rationale of the gift economy, some participants make contributions without expecting any monetary compensation. In this connection, a key factor that motivates participants is a strong sense of group identification (see Chapter 6). Hertel et al. (2003) studied the case of Linux and pointed out that the more users identified themselves as Linux developers, the more involved they became and the more effort they put into developing the relative code. The reputation they gained and the positive image the project continued to reinforce over time increased the sense of responsibility and trust between the programmers as well as the feeling of being useful to their peers. Finally, another important motivation of a social nature is the determination to carry out campaigns to 'fight against proprietary software'.

A third category refers to incentives of a technological nature such as learning,[5] the contributions and feedback of other users, and the possibility of working with a new technology rather than solving problems of personal interest.

Although up until now the incentives to motivate participation have referred to the benefits that individuals can obtain by participating in OSS, it is also worth mentioning the specific advantages that firms can enjoy if they develop collective innovation processes using open-source software. While the classic incentives to innovation are economic, related mainly to licenses and royalties that protect income through the traditional systems of intellectual property rights, the incentives that exploit the dynamics of OSS are basically different and include lower transaction costs and positive network effects.

It is also worth noting that this etherarchical organizational model that supports distributed innovation has its origin, as well as its principal development, in the software market and in digital goods or goods that can be digitalized, such as videogames. However, this does not mean that applications cannot be extended to other sectors that would like to develop physical products, such as sports clothing (von Hippel, 2001). As in the case of the communities created to develop software, the ones dedicated to physical products range from simple support sites to the exchange of information – such as the communities of interest described in Chapter 6 – up to veritable communities equipped with tools and infrastructures to support innovation. For example, Franke and Shah (2003) study the relatively simple infrastructure of a 'boardercross community' made up from semi-professional athletes from all over the world that meet up to ten times a year to race in international competitions in Europe, North America and Japan. The members know each other very well and spend a lot of time together. Moreover, they help each other develop and modify their sports equipment though no special tools have been created to support collaborative innovation. In fact, what clearly emerges from the study is that the members most willing to support and assist the others are also those who make contributions to innovation (Tables 8.3 and 8.4).

There are, however, communities that focus attention on developing physical products with structures that are much more complex and reproduce the richness and refinement of OSS, including analogous tools and infrastructural devices. This is exemplified by a recently established community that aims to develop and diffuse information regarding equipment for kitesurfing, a water sport that uses a board, similar to a surfboard, attached to a power kite that pulls the kitesurfer through the water (von Hippel, 2005). Developing this equipment requires great technical skills and knowledge of low-speed aerodynamics that is still not fully developed. The first kites were developed and built by enthusiastic fans who also developed kitesurfing instructions and equipment design. In 2001 a student at MIT and enthusiastic kitesurfer decided to establish a virtual community – www.zeroprestige.com – dedicated to all those who wanted to contribute suggestions for improvements. Many of the users who joined proved to have considerable technical skills which they made available to the community, sharing their own kite models, and providing suggestions on how to build sophisticated support equipment, such as software to design aerodynamic models and rapid prototypes.

The basic assumption that makes it possible to adopt OSS even in these environments is that during the development stage all products are information products. The techniques of computer-aided design that have

Table 8.3   Number of users that provide assistance to innovators

Number of users	Number of cases	Percentage
0	0	0
1	3	6
2	14	26
3–5	25	47
6–10	8	15
> 10	3	6
Total	53	100

Source: Adapted from Franke and Shah (2003).

Table 8.4   Reciprocal assistance among the innovators: a comparison

	Innovators	Non-innovators	Total
Provide assistance	28	13	41
Do not provide assistance	32	115	147
Total	60	128	

Source: Adapted from Franke and Shah (2003).

become so popular in supporting NPD emphasize its transformation into information that is shared on a large scale. In the case of the kitesurfer community, the time required to convert an information product into a physical product was usually less than a week, whereas the total cost of a kite developed in this way was much less than the normal price of a kite sold on the market (von Hippel, 2005). These kinds of applications are still in their infancy, but undoubtedly represent one of the principal challenges that OSS have to face to increase even further their importance as a tool that can act as a catalyst in collaborative innovation processes.

NOTES

1. The theory of the gift economy originated well before the theory of the Net. Mauss (1959) was among the first to formalize it.
2. Raymond (1999) cleverly summed up this principle by coining the so-called 'Law of Linux': 'Given enough eyeballs, all bugs are shallow'.
3. Of the seven strategies, this one is the most controversial since project contributors transfer their individual rights to non-profit foundations in order to protect these rights, but no project requires these rights to be transferred as a necessary condition. The GNU and Apache projects are the most active in promoting – but not imposing – the transfer of the programmer's *copyright* to non-profit organizations.
4. The Apache software has, for example, been transferred to the Apache Software Foundation.
5. Lakhani and von Hippel (2000), for example, identify two different typologies of users in the Apache developer community: the 'provider' and the 'seeker' of knowledge. The main objective of the participation is learning and the provider is the one that usually finds the answers.

9. Conclusions

This book has shed light on the key drivers of collaborative innovation in a context where NPD activities assume a more and more distributed nature. It has highlighted the new tools that companies can use in order to collaborate with their customers in digital settings and it has sketched out three major organizational modes of collaborative innovation in the extended network. At the same time, it has contributed to identifying two fundamental dilemmas, which we would like to leave at the end of our book as food for thought for scholars interested in the field.

9.1 THE KNOWLEDGE DILEMMA: SPECIALIZATION VERSUS MULTIDISCIPLINARITY

A first dilemma associated with value creation in collaborative innovation is related to the fact that ICTs increase the need for knowledge specialization both at the firm and at the community level, but at the same time they require the development of more diverse competences to face convergent industries, generating possibilities of reconnection and recombination through both weak and strong virtual ties. To some extent, ICTs simultaneously create the 'problem' – knowledge specialization – and its 'solution' – knowledge socialization. However, the likelihood of success in matching these opposite drivers depends on the firm's ability to select the proper combination between the lead sponsor of the value creation activity and the tightness of the linkages connecting all the actors of the collaborative innovation system. Hence, in order to drive this decision proficiently, managers need to be provided not only with the entire portfolio of alternative governance modes, but also with some specific contingent factors for different value creation mechanisms. Future research can enhance the comprehension of their portfolio, which includes several components.

A first critical factor in driving the firm's choice of a specific value creation mode can be represented by the level of knowledge modularity. When applied to knowledge creation, modularity can be gained by decomposing the knowledge required in the innovation process into modules that must be first produced and then combined. Consequently, in a collaborative innovation system some actors can focus on the production of knowledge modules and benefit from economies of scale, while others can focus on combining and adapting these modules of knowledge to use them at the firm level. When there is a need for intense modularity – for instance, to develop complex digital products – flexible organizations are required and collaboration has to be especially extended. Different pieces of knowledge need to be recombined and variously integrated on a contingent basis. A highly structured organization is not coherent with such a goal. Intense coordination reduces flexibility. Moreover, when the sponsor of the value creation activity is a community, a higher variety of knowledge modules can be leveraged.

The opportunity to pool a heterogeneous set of resources today also seems to be substantially increased by the fragmentation of markets. In fragmented markets, knowledge tends to be variously distributed among different sources and to become embedded in the shared infrastructure connecting such sources. As a consequence, the need for re-aggregation and rewiring increases. In other words, there is a need for a 'free market' for ideas and resources to support them, which enhance the opportunities to exploit resource heterogeneity.

The level of industry dynamism pushes in a similar direction. The more intense the rate of change of a specific industry, the higher the need for the company to leverage open systems for collaborative innovation. In fact, poorly structured ties allow the firm to continuously redefine the portfolio of relationships it has developed in order to support a distributed innovation system, on the basis of emerging knowledge needs. As we have argued in this book, the rapid pace of change and the uncertainty of the nature of change in dynamic markets require firms to look beyond their immediate field of view, if they want to avoid the core rigidities that result from self-referential learning. Dynamic market settings also require firms to continually reconfigure their organizational architecture so that they can generate double-loop learning (Argyris and Schön, 1978). In these settings, firms need to continuously absorb knowledge and transform such knowledge into new products (Teece et al., 1997). This is also true in nascent markets where customer needs are poorly understood and evolve rapidly. In such contexts, firms need to rapidly sequence new products (Helfat and Raubitschek, 2000) and continuously introduce innovations (Eisenhardt and Martin, 2000). To support this pace of innovation, firms need to tap into additional sources of knowledge and expand their span for collaboration with the periphery.

Proximity dependence (or task decomposability) is a further contingent factor. When it is high, value creation tasks cannot be easily separated. In the opposite situation, when proximity independence prevails, different players can accomplish remotely different tasks, simultaneously cooperating with a superior joint innovative output.

Finally, the complexity of the innovative task to be pursued represents another contingent factor that requires to be taken into careful consideration. When the total cost – that is, the total risk – associated with the project is especially high, the individual firm needs to maintain a strong control on the entire process, and it cannot afford to make undirected innovative efforts. Hence, it also tends to maintain the role of the lead sponsor of the entire value creation process, creating strict rules and requirements for collaboration.

More broadly, research should further highlight the correlation between the number of involved actors, the degree of openness of the collaborative innovation process, and the level of coordination maintained by the sponsor company. When the actors contributing to collaborative innovation – notwithstanding its lead sponsor – are limited in number, it might seem to be more proficient to rely on structured ties and formal coordination mechanisms, in order to enhance the efficiency of the process. Specifically, the more open and organic the process, the higher the creativity and the variety of the knowledge inputs, but also the greater the difficulty in capturing rents. Hence, an organic approach could probably be preferred at the idea generation stage, when serendipity and creative chaos can play a major role in supporting the innovative effort. At this stage, too much dependency among different knowledge modules could reduce the degrees of freedom in their recombination and, thereby, prevent disruptive ideas from developing. In addition, the company needs to increase the level of coordination among its innovation activities. Monetary investments are required to take further steps into the innovation process and investors need to be sure about actual returns. As a consequence, a more structured approach could be more properly adopted at these advanced stages, in order to enhance the likelihood of finalizing the process of distributed innovation proficiently.

These and other contingencies might be explored in more depth in future research, in order to identify specific guidelines to drive managerial choices related to the proper organization of collaborative innovation.

9.2   THE INCENTIVE DILEMMA: COPYRIGHT VERSUS COPYLEFT

Moving on from the traditional closed mode of innovation towards forms of distributed and collaborative innovation, firms also face new challenges for capturing the rent from innovation. In fact, traditional closed models of innovation were also protected by the legal tools that have been developed throughout the years for strengthening the economically fragile nature of knowledge. The current system of intellectual property rights aims at protecting the innovation rent from the potential free riders (for example, Arora et al., 2001). Yet, the emerging collaborative approach demands new answers. More precisely, a second dilemma emerges in a system of distributed innovation. Creativity and innovation are fuelled by past intellectual activity. Hence, the higher the openness of the system and the tolerated level of serendipity, the stronger the impulse to knowledge creation and innovation. However, free dissemination of intellectual works also prevents the creators from benefiting from their endeavors, and can potentially create a 'tragedy of the commons', where nobody retains the motivation to create new intellectual property, and everybody aims to exploit others' intellectual property.

In the traditional proprietary approach, all intellectual property created is owned by a single firm, which extracts rents by licensing or otherwise exploiting it. In contrast, in open innovation systems, a completely anarchic 'marketplace of ideas' tends to prevail. No individual entity owns the intellectual property that is created. Creators enjoy a wide range of freedoms, but they are also vulnerable to exploitation. Distributed innovation systems need to find a balance out of these two extremes in intellectual property rights management. Specifically, a new equilibrium has to be identified as to how intellectual property rights are vested and how rents are extracted at both the individual and organizational levels, in order to make the collaborative innovation system able to self-sustain on time.

While legal tools are rapidly trying to catch up with the new challenging questions, it is clear that firms also need to embrace new strategies. Specifically, we can identify different types of incentives supporting systematic contribution in distributed innovation. When a firm directly develops a specific innovation it can protect the rent stemming from it through the copyright system – and hence with a specific patent or license, demanding royalties for its innovations. In this case, the company obviously relies on its proprietary advantage; contracts embody the spirit of the collaboration or the 'ground rules' that parties – two to many – use to govern the distributed innovation system. These types of contracts usually specify who contributes what to the system, who gets credit for what, what each party gets out of the contract, and for how long parties agree to collaborate under these rules. Contracts allow economic rights to be separated from property rights for a predetermined period.

When a single person creates the rent through the development of valuable knowledge, he/she can protect the innovation directly through the copyright system or, if working for a corporation, can gain a direct benefit through the salary earned and the bonuses that are typically linked to such achievements. In other words, this is an incentive system based on reward for innovation. For instance, in the Whirlpool Corporation, the 30 per cent of Unit General Managers' evaluation and compensation is based on their innovation output, while in Herman Miller those ideas that proceed from the generation stage through to the market stage are rewarded with increasing financial bonuses.

A completely different type of incentive is represented by attribution, which is very important for any participant operating in a market where reputation can be considered the main currency. When a single person participates in a system of pure distributed innovation, it is clear that he/she does not directly gain under the economic viewpoint from the knowledge produced and shared. The management of intellectual property rights has in fact been revolutionized by collaborative and open innovation mechanisms, leading to the so-called 'copyleft' principle (von Hippel and von Krogh, 2003). Hence, the typical gain in this case has to do with the reputation of the person. In fact, individuals can substantially improve their reputation and hence their prestige with the ratings in specific websites and with the overall citations they might receive for their inventions. In so far as the quality of a patent is measured by the number of citations it receives, the number of citations and the ranking in OSS contributes to a person's general reputation, according to a peer-group recognition principle. As a consequence, this type of incentive is usually associated with mechanisms of value creation that are enhanced through the presence of a community of developers, where ties among parties tend to be more organic, and gaining visibility and reputation play a major role in defining the quality of individual contributions to the community. For instance, in BioMed Central (www.biomedcentral.com), any participant is free to copy, distribute and display any available contribution; to make derivative works; and to make commercial use of the same works, but only if he/she respects some very specific requirements: the original author has to be given credit for any reuse or distribution, and the license terms of this work must be made clear to others. These conditions can be waived only if the authors give explicit permission.

Incentives can also be associated with lower transaction costs. More precisely, access to a wide range of community technologies via a single transaction is more efficient than many transactions with each member of a large community, as we can argue from the original work of Coase and Demsetz. This type of incentive usually works well when the company can selectively enact relationships with particular communities that can provide a specific contribution to fill in contingent knowledge gaps. The same incentive can also partially work when the company decides to internalize the community of developers and to act as the leading sponsor of the distributed innovation process.

Finally, participants in a distributed innovation system may be motivated by the benefits deriving from vicarious network effects. In certain networked markets, broader exposure to offerings of other community members may allow firms to take advantage of both direct and indirect network externalities and other network effects. Specifically, direct network externalities can be related to the opportunity of accessing a wider range of development resources and intellectual property contributed by other participants. Analogously, interaction with community members may lead to new market access for the individual. Indirect network externalities can instead be associated with two further types of incentives: predatory commoditization and complementary services. More specifically, the system of incentives is especially threatened when it is the firm that contributes indirectly to the creation of the rent. For instance, it is unlikely that the commitment of many of the R&D personnel of a corporation who spend most of their time in solving specific challenges in an OSS website can be understood with the traditional rationale. Indeed, the type of gain the firm tries to capture is related to the strategy that we have called 'predatory commoditization'. For instance, in order to gain from the innovation, a software company can eliminate the rent from a specific software application and transfer it to other related services that will be bought by those people who will download the software. Thus the firm changes not only the rules of the game, but even the same game: instead of playing to win the software battle, it moves the battlefield to the service behind the software usage. In other words, in predatory commoditization the individual company aggressively commoditizes a part of the value chain on which its other competitors strongly depend.

A slightly different alternative within this approach is to work on complementary services, in order to gain lower innovation and support costs. For example, MySQL has used copyrights and patents to protect its product, while developing software that has gained acceptance by the development community. While MySQL is branded as open source, it maintains ownership and copyright control of its software. The firm is leveraging its copyrights and trademarks to further develop its brand and it is now viewed as the open-source alternative in the database market. Specifically, it is riding the open-source wave to penetrate the database market by pricing its products below proprietary rivals. MySQL is targeting traditionally high-margin database add-on products, such as clusters, and is pricing software well below its larger rivals. It uses the open-source community to lower its cost base by 'outsourcing' the labor-intensive functions of testing and documentation.

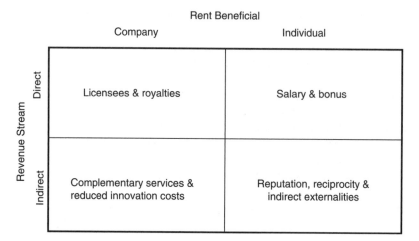

Figure 9.1   Mapping the incentives supporting collaborative innovation

Figure 9.1 synthesizes the four incentive schemes. Each type of incentive clearly presents some distinguishing features that make it more suitable to prize individual contributions and support rent appropriation under different archetypes of value creation in a context of distributed and collaborative innovation. Hence, firms need to discover the best combination of rent appropriation mechanisms according to the specific problem they face in value creation. More precisely, direct payoffs tend to have an economic nature and appear to be preferred by those companies that maintain a strong and rigid coordination of their collaborative effort. In contrast, indirect payoffs seem to be mainly related to externalities mediated through other phenomena, and to be more properly associated with truly open and dispersed collaborative approaches.

In any case, these new rules for rent appropriation in collaborative settings open up a promising new area for future research, in order to further explore how intellectual property rights are vested, and how rents can be extracted at both the individual and organizational levels, in order to make the collaborative innovation system self-sustainable on time.

In conclusion, in this book our premise has been to understand why collaborative innovation with customers is relevant and how it works. Now the challenge is to expand our research in order to help companies to face the daily pitfalls they might meet in implementing collaborative innovation on a systematic basis, starting from the contingencies that can drive their collaborative approaches and the incentives they have to provide in order to motivate all the potential contributors to make a joint effort. In line with our perspective, real innovation is today driven by an ecosystem of various players, who collaborate and add value to a shared discussion. The contribution of each one, including the sponsor firm, supplements the others, beyond any cultural, geographical and organizational boundary or barrier. Future research has to help companies to design an ecosystem in which customers play an increasingly fundamental role; however, they are, of course, not the only actors in the field.

References

Afuah, A. (2003), 'Redefining firm boundaries in the face of the Internet: are firms really shrinking?', *Academy of Management Review*, **28** (1): 34–53.

Afuah, A. and Tucci, C. (2000), *Internet Business Models and Strategies: Text and Cases*, New York: McGraw-Hill.

Aghion, P. and Tirole, J. (1994), 'The management of innovation', *Quarterly Journal of Economic*, **109** (4), November: 1185–209.

Ahuja, G. (2000), 'Collaboration networks, structural holes, and innovation: a longitudinal study', *Administrative Science Quarterly*, **45**: 425–55.

Alba, J., Lynch, J., Weitz, B., Janiszewski, C., Lutz, R., Sawyer, A. and Wood, S. (1997), 'Interactive home shopping: consumer, retailer, and manufacturer incentives to participate in electronic marketplaces', *Journal of Marketing*, **61** (3): 38–53.

Anand, V., Manz, C.C. and Glick, W.H. (1998), 'An organisational memory approach to information management', *Academy of Management Review*, **23** (4): 796–809.

Andal-Ancion, A., Cartwright, P.A. and Yip, G.S. (2003), 'The digital transformation of traditional businesses', *MIT Sloan Management Review*, Summer: 34–41.

Anderson, W.L. and Crocca, W.T. (1993), 'Engineering practice and co-development of product prototypes', *Communications of the ACM*, **36** (4): 49–56.

Antorini, Y.M. (2005), 'Analysis of the adult fans of Lego Users' group', paper presented at the I MIT User Group Conference, 27–29 June, Sloan Management School, Boston, MA.

Argyris, C. and Schön, D. (1978), *Organizational Learning II: Theory, Method and Practice*, Reading, MA: Addison-Wesley.

Armstrong, A. and Hagel, J. III (1996), 'The real value of online communities', *Harvard Business Review*, May–June: 134–41.

Arnould, E.J. and Price, L.L. (1993), 'River magic: extraordinary experience and the extended service encounter', *Journal of Consumer Research*, **20**: 24–45.

Arora, A., Fosfuri, A. and Gambardella, A. (2001), *Markets for Technology: The Economics of Innovation and Corporate Strategy*, Cambridge, MA: MIT Press.

Arora, A. and Gambardella, A. (1994), 'The changing technology of technological change. General and abstract knowledge and the division of innovative labour', *Research Policy*, **23**: 523–32.

Austin, R.D. (2001), 'The effects of time pressure on quality in software development: an agency model', *Information Systems Research*, **12** (2): 195–207.

Bagozzi, R.P. and Dholakia, U.M. (2002), 'Intentional social action in virtual communities', *Journal of Interactive Marketing*, **16** (2): 2–21.

Bakos, Y. (1997), 'Reducing buyer search cost: implications for electronic marketplaces', *Management Science*, **43** (12): 1676–92.

Balasubramanian, S., Krishnan, V. and Sawhney, M. (1998), 'The implications of digitization for markets and marketing', Working Paper, Kellogg School of Management, Northwestern University, Chicago, IL.

Baldwin, C.Y. and Clark, K.B. (1992), 'Capabilities and capital investment: new perspectives on capital budgeting', *Journal of Applied Corporate Finance*, **5** (2) (Summer): 67–87.

Baldwin, C.Y. and Clark, K.B. (1997), 'Managing in an age of modularity', *Harvard Business Review*, September–October: 84–93.

Bardakci, A. and Whitelock, J. (2004), 'How ready are customers for mass customization? An exploratory investigation', *European Journal of Marketing*, **38** (11/12): 1396–416.

Beaubien, M.P. (1996), 'Playing at community: multi-user dungeons and social interaction in cyberspace', in L. Strate, R. Jacobsen and S.B. Gibson (eds), *Communication and Cyberspace: Social Interaction in an Electronic Environment*, Cresskill, NJ: Hampton Press, pp. 179–89.

Bendapudi, N. and Leone, R.P. (2003), 'Psychological implications of customer participation in co-production', *Journal of Marketing*, **67** (January): 14–28.

Bergquist, M. and Ljungberg, J. (2001), 'The power of gifts: organising social relationships in Open Source communities', *European Journal of Information Systems*, **11** (4): 305–20.

Berthon, P., Holbrook, M.B. and Hulbert, J.M. (2000), 'Beyond market orientation: a conceptualization of market evolution', *Journal of Interactive Marketing*, **14** (3): 50–66.

Bezroukov, N. (1999), 'Open Source software development as a special type of academic research (critique of the vulgar raymondism)', http://www.firstmonday.dk/issues/issue4_10/bezroukov.

Bhattacharya, C.B. and Sen, S. (2003), 'Consumer–company identification: a framework for understanding consumers' relationships with companies', *Journal of Marketing*, **67** (April): 76–88.

Bhattacharya, S., Krishnan, V. and Mahajan, V. (1998), 'Managing new product definition in highly dynamic environments', *Management Science*, **40**: 50–64.

Bickart, B. and Schindler, R.M. (2001), 'Internet forums as influential sources of consumer information', *Journal of Interactive Marketing*, **15** (3): 31–40.

Böhme, G. (1997), 'The structures and prospects of knowledge society', *Social Science. Information sur les sciences sociales*, **3**: 447–68.

Boland, R.J. and Tenkasi, R. (1995), 'Perspective making and perspective taking in communities of knowing', *Organization Science*, **6**: 350–72.

Bonaccorsi, A. and Rossi, C. (2003), 'Why Open Source software can succeed', *Research Policy*, **32** (1): 1243–58.

Booz, Allen & Hamilton (1968), *Management of New Products*, Chicago, IL: Booz, Allen & Hamilton.

Booz, Allen & Hamilton (1982), *New Product Management for the 1980's*, Chicago, IL: Booz, Allen & Hamilton.

Bowen, D.E. (1986), 'Managing customers as human resources in service organizations', *Human Resource Management*, **25** (3): 371–83.

Brandenburger, A. and Nalebuff, B. (1996), *Co-opetition*, New York: Doubleday.

Brown, J.S. and Duguid, P. (1991), 'Organizational learning and communities of practice: toward a unified view of working, learning and innovation', *Organization Science*, **2**: 40–57.

Brown, J.S. and Duguid, P. (2000), *The Social Life of Information*, Boston, MA: Harvard Business School Press.

Brown, S.L. and Eisenhardt, K.M. (1995), 'Product development: past research, present findings, and future directions', *Academy of Management Review*, **20**: 343–78.

Brown, S.L. and Eisenhardt, K.M. (1998), *Competing on the Edge*, Boston, MA: Harvard Business School Press.

Brynjolfsson, E. and Smith, M.D. (2000), 'Frictionless commerce? A comparison of Internet and conventional retailers', *Management Science*, **46** (4): 563–85.

Bughin, J. and Manyika, J. (2007), 'How Businesses are using Web 2.0, McKinsey Global Survey 2007', *McKinsey Quarterly*, July: 1–7.

Burgess, R. (1982), 'The unreconstructed interview as a conversation', in R. Burgess (ed.) *A Sourcebook and Field Manual*, London: Allen & Unwin, pp. 107–10.

Burke, R.R., Rangaswamy, A. and Gupta, S. (2001), 'Rethinking market research in the digital world', in J. Wind and V. Mahajan (eds), *Digital Marketing: Global Strategies from the World's Leading Experts*, New York: John Wiley & Sons, pp. 226–55.

Burt, R.S. (1992), *Structural Holes: The Social Structure of Competition*, Boston, MA: Harvard Business School Press.

Carmel, E., Whitaker, R.D. and George, J.F. (1993), 'PD and joint application design: a transatlantic comparison', *Communication of the ACM*, **36** (4): 40–48.

Carraca, J. and Carrilho, M.M. (1996), 'The role of sharing in circulation of knowledge', *Futures*, **28** (8): 771–9.

Cartwright, E. (2002), 'Learning to play approximate Nash equilibria in games with many players', Levine's Working Paper Archive 506439000000000070, UCLA Department of Economics.

Castaldo, S., Troilo, G., Verona, G. and Bertozzi, P. (1995), 'Networks for Innovation', Proceedings IMP Group Conference (September), Manchester, UK.

Chatterjee, P. (2001), 'Online reviews: do consumers use them?', in M.C. Gilli and J. Myers-Levi (eds), *Advances in Consumer Research*, vol. 28, Provo, UT: Association for Consumer Research, pp. 129–33.

Chesbrough, H.W. (2003), 'The era of open innovation', *MIT Sloan Management Review*, Spring: 35–41.

Chesbrough, H.W. (2005), *Open Innovation*, Boston, MA: Harvard Business School Press.

Chesbrough, H. (2006), 'Open innovation: a new paradigm for understanding industrial innovation', in H. Chesbrough, W. Vanhaverbeke and J. West (eds), *Open Innovation: Researching a New Paradigm*, Oxford: Oxford University Press, pp. 1–12.

Christensen, C.M. (1997), *The Innovator's Dilemma: When New Technologies Cause Great Firms to Fail*, Boston, MA: Harvard Business School Press.

Christensen, C.M. and Bower, J.L. (1996), 'Customer power, strategic investment, and the failure of leading firms', *Strategic Management Journal*, **17**: 197–218.

Clark, K.B. and Fujimoto, T. (1991), *Product Development Performance*, Boston, MA: Harvard Business School Press.

Coase, R.H. (1937), 'The nature of the firm', *Economica*, **4** (n.s.) (November): 386–405.

Cockburn, I.M., Henderson, R. and Stern, S. (2000), 'Untangling the origins of competitive advantage', *Strategic Management Journal*, **21**: 1123–45.

Cohen, W.M. and Levinthal, D.A. (1990), 'Absorptive capacity: a new perspective on learning and innovation', *Administrative Science Quarterly*, **35**: 128–52.

Constant, D., Sproull, L. and Kiesler, S. (1996), 'The kindness of strangers: the usefulness of electronic weak ties for technical advice organization science', *Organization Science*, **7** (2): 119–35.

Coombs, R. and Metcalfe, J.S. (2000), 'Organizing for innovation: co-ordinating distributed innovation capabilities', in J.N. Foss and V. Mahnke (eds), *Competence, Governance, and Entrepreneurship*, Oxford: Oxford University Press, pp. 209–31.

Cooper, R.G. (1988), 'The new product process: a decision guide for management', *Journal of Marketing Management*, **3** (3): 238–55.

Craincross, F. (1997), *The Death of Distance: How the Communication Revolution Will Change Our Lives*, Boston, MA: Harvard Business School Press.

Crawford, C. and Benedetto, A. (2006), *New Products Marketing*, New York: McGraw Hill.

Cusumano, M.A. (1992), 'Shifting economies: from craft production to flexible systems and software factories', *Research Policy*, **21** (5): 453–80.

Cusumano, M.A. (1997), 'How Microsoft makes large teams work like small teams', *Sloan Management Review*, **39**: 9–21.

Czepiel, John A. (1990), 'Service encounters and service relationships: implications for research', *Journal of Business Research*, **20** (1), 13–21.

Dahan, E. and Hauser, J. (2002), 'Product development – managing a dispersed process', in B. Weitz and R. Wensley (eds), *Handbook of Marketing*, Thousand Oaks, CA: Sage, pp. 179–222.

Dahan, E. and Srinivasan 'Seenu', V. (2000), 'The predictive power of Internet-based product concept testing using virtual depiction and animation', *Journal of Product Innovation Management*, **17** (March): 99–109.

Dalle, J.M. and David, P.A. (2003), 'The allocation of software development resources in "open source" production mode', MIT Working Paper, Boston, MA.

Danneels, E. (2003), 'Tight–loose coupling with customers: the enactment of customers' orientation', *Strategic Management Journal*, **24**: 559–76.

Davenport, T.H. and Prusak, L. (1998), *Working Knowledge: How Organizations Manage What They Know*, Boston, MA: Harvard Business School Press.

David, K. and Pfaff, B. (1998), 'Society and Open Source: why Open Source software is better for society than closed source software', http://www.msu.edn/user/pfaffben/writings/anp/oss-is-better.html.

Day, G.S. (1994), 'The capabilities of market-driven organization', *Journal of Marketing*, **58**: 37–52.

Day, G.S. (1998), 'Organizing for interactivity', *Journal of Interactive Marketing*, **12** (1): 47–53.

Day, G.S. (2000), 'Managing market relationships', *Journal of the Academy of Marketing Science*, **28** (1): 24–30.

Day, G.S. and Wensley, R. (1988), 'Assessing advantage: a framework for diagnosing competitive superiority', *Journal of Marketing*, **52**: 1–20.

Demsetz, H. (1967), 'Towards a theory of property rights', *American Economic Review*, 57: 347–59.

Denzin, N. (1997), *Interpretive Ethnography: Ethnographic Practices for the 21st Century*, Thousand Oaks, CA: Sage.

Di Bernardo, B. and Rullani, E. (1990), *Il Management e le Macchine*, Bologna: Il Mulino.

Di Bona, C., Ockman, S. and Stone, M. (eds) (1999), *Open Source: Voices from the Open Source Revolution*, Sebastopol, CA: O'Reilly.

Doering, D.S. and Parayre, R. (2000), 'Identification and assessment of emerging technologies', in G.S. Day and P.J.H. Shoemaker (eds), *Wharton on Managing Emerging Technologies*, New York: John Wiley & Sons, pp. 75–98.

Donath, B. (1992), 'The customer as consultant', *Sales and Marketing Management*, September: 84–90.

Dougherty, D. (1992), 'Interpretative barriers to successful product innovation in large firms', *Organization Science*, **3**: 179–202.

Douglas, M. and Isherwood, B. (1979), *The World of Goods*, New York: Basic Books.

Downes, L. and Mui, C. (1998), *Unleashing the Killer App: Digital Strategies for Market Dominance*, Boston, MA: Harvard Business School Press.

Dyer, J.H. and Nobeoka, K. (2000), 'Creating and managing a high-performance knowledge-sharing network: the Toyota case', *Strategic Management Journal*, **21**: 345–67.

Eisenhardt, K.M. (1989), 'Building theories from case study research', *Academy of Management Review*, **14** (4): 532–50.

Eisenhardt, K.M. and Martin, J.A. (2000), 'Dynamic capabilities: what are they?', *Strategic Management Journal*, **21** (10–11): 1105–21.

Eisenhardt, K.M. and Tabrizi, B.N. (1995), 'Accelerating adaptive processes: product innovation in the global computer industry', *Administrative Science Quarterly*, **40** (1): 84–110.

Evans, P. and Wurster, T. (1997), 'Strategy and the new economics of information', *Harvard Business Review*, **75** (5): 71–82.

Evans, P. and Wurster, T. (1999), *Blown to Bits: How the New Economics of Information Transforms Strategy*, Boston, MA: Harvard Business School Press.

Fahey, L. and Prusak, L. (1999), 'The eleven deadliest sins of knowledge management', *California Management Review*, **40** (3), Spring: 265–75.

Feldman, M. (1995), *Strategies for Interpreting Qualitative Data*, Thousand Oaks, CA: Sage.

Feller, J. and Fitzgerald, B. (2002), *Understanding Open Source Software Development*, Boston, MA: Addison-Wesley.

Fielding, R. (1999), 'Shared leadership in the Apache project', *Communications of the ACM*, **42** (4): 42–3.

Firat, A.F. and Venkatesh, A. (1995), 'Liberatory postmodernism and the reenchantment of consumption', *Journal of Consumer Research*, **22**, December: 239–67.

Firat, A.F., Dholakia, N. and Venkatesh, A. (1995), 'Marketing in a Postmodern World', *European Journal of Marketing*, **29** (1): 40–56.

Franke, N. and von Hippel, E. (2003), 'Satisfying heterogeneous user needs via innovation toolkits: the case of Apache security software', *Research Policy*, **32** (1): 157–78.

Franke, N. and Shah, S. (2003), 'How communities support innovative activities: an exploration of assistance and sharing among end-users', *Research Policy*, **31** (1): 157–78.

Galimberti, C., Ignazi, S., Vercesi, P. and Riva, G. (2001), 'Communication and cooperation in networked environments: an experimental analysis', *CyberPsychology and Behavior*, **4** (1): 131–46.

Gambardella, A. and Rullani, E. (1999), 'Divisione del Lavoro Tecnologico e Media di Condivisione della Conoscenza: Alla Ricerca di Nuove Istituzioni', *Economia e Politica Industriale*, 101–2.

Garbarino, E. and Johnson, M.S. (1999), 'The different role of satisfaction, trust, and commitment in customer relationships', *Journal of Marketing*, **63** (April): 70–87.

Garton, L., Haythornthwaite, C. and Wellman, B. (1997), 'Studying online social networks', *Journal of Computer-Mediated Communication*, **3** (1): 75–105.

Garud, R., Kumaraswamy, A. and Langlois, R.N. (eds) (2002), *Managing in the Modular Age: Architectures, Networks, and Organizations*, Oxford: Blackwell.

Gavetti, G. and Levinthal, D.A. (2000), 'Looking forward and looking backward: cognitive and experiential search', *Administrative Science Quarterly*, **45** (1): 113–37.

Giuri, P., Ploner, M., Rullani, F. and Torrisi, S. (2007), 'An explorative study of skills and openness in Open Source software projects, *Sinergie*, **26**: 275–87.

Gladwell, M. (2000), *The Tipping Point: How Little Things Can Make a Big Difference*, Boston, MA: Little, Brown.

Glaser, B. and Strauss, A. (1967), *The Discovery of Grounded Theory*, Chicago, IL: Aldine.

Godbout, J.T. and Caillé, A. (1992), *L'Esprit du Don*, Paris: La Découverte.

Godin, S. (1999), *Permission Marketing: Turning Strangers into Friends, and Friends into Customers*, New York: Simon & Schuster.

Goldman, A.I. (1999), *Knowledge in a Social World*, Oxford: Oxford University Press.

Goodwin, C. (1994), 'Private roles in public encounters: communal relationships in service exchanges', *Proceedings of the 3rd Seminaire International de Recherche en Management des Activités de Services*, La Londe les Maures, May: 311–33.

Govindarajan, V. and Trimble, C. (2006), 'Ten rules for strategic innovators: from idea to execution', *Journal of Product Innovation Management*, **23** (5): 466–7.

Granitz, N.A. and Ward, J.C. (1996), 'Virtual community: a sociocognitive analysis', in *Advances in Consumer Research*, **23**: 161–6.

Green, L.G. (2000), 'Economics of Open Source software', http://badtux. org/home/eric/editorial/economics.php.

Gulati, R. (1999), 'Network location and learning: the influence of network resources and firm capabilities on alliance formation', *Strategic Management Journal*, **20** (5): 397–420.

Gulati, R. and Gargiulo, M. (1999), 'Where do interorganizational networks come from?', *American Journal of Sociology*, **104** (5): 1439–93.

Gulati, R., Nohria, N. and Zahere, A. (2000), 'Strategic networks', *Strategic Management Journal*, **21**: 203–15.

Gummeson, E. (1998), 'Implementation requires a relationship marketing paradigm', *Journal of the Academy of Marketing Science*, **26** (3): 242–9.

Hagel, J., III (1999), 'Net gain: expanding markets through virtual communities', *Journal of Interactive Marketing*, **13** (1): 55–65.

Hagel, J., III and Armstrong, A.G. (1997), *Net Gain: Expanding Markets Through Virtual Communities*, Boston, MA: Harvard Business School Press.

Hagel, J. and Rayport, J.F. (1997), 'The coming battle for customer information', *Harvard Business Review*, **75** (1): 5–11.

Hagel, J. and Singer, M. (1999), *Net Worth: Shaping Markets When Customers Make the Rules*, Boston, MA: Harvard Business School Press.

Hamel, G. and Prahalad, C.K. (1994), *Competing for the Future*, Boston, MA: Harvard Business School Press.

Hamm, S. (2005), 'Linux, Inc.', *Business Week,* January 31, http://www. businessweek.com/magazine/content/05_05/63918001_m2001.htm.

Hansen, M.T., Nohria, N. and Tierney, T. (1999), 'What's your strategy for managing knowledge?', *Harvard Business Review*, March–April: 106–16.

Hargadon, A.B. (1998), 'Firms as knowledge brokers: lessons in pursuing continuous innovation', *California Management Review*, **40** (3): 209–27.

Hargadon, A.B. (2003), *How Breakthroughs Happen: The Surprising Truth about How Companies Innovate*, Boston, MA: Harvard Business School Press.

Hargadon, A.B. and Sutton, R. (1997), 'Technology brokering and innovation in a product-development firm', *Administrative Science Quarterly*, **42**: 716–49.

Hargadon, A.B. and Sutton, R. (2000), 'Building an innovation factory', *Harvard Business Review*, May–June: 157–66.

Hauser, J.R. and Clausing, D. (1988), 'The house of quality', *Harvard Business Review*, May–June: 63–73.

Hauser, J., Tellis, G.J. and Griffin, A. (2007), 'Research on innovation and new products: a review and agenda for marketing science', *Marketing Science*, **25** (6): 687–717.

Hayes, R.H., Wheelwright, S. and Clark, K. (1988), *Dynamic Manufacturing: Creating the Learning Organization*, New York: Free Press.

Hecker, F. (1999), 'Setting up shop: the business of open-source software', *IEEE Software*, January/February: 45–51.

Helfat, C.E. and Raubitschek, R.S. (2000), 'Product sequencing: co-evolution of knowledge, capabilities and products', *Strategic Management Journal*, **21**: 961–79.

Hennig-Thurau, T., Gwinner, K.P., Walsh, G. and Gremler, D.D. (2004), 'Electronic word-of-mouth via consumer-opinion platforms: what motivates consumers to articulate themselves on the Internet?', *Journal of Interactive Marketing*, **18** (1), 38–52.

Herr, P.M., Kardes, F.R. and Kim, J. (1991), 'Effects of word-of-mouth and product-attribute information on persuasion: an accessibility-diagnostic perspective', *Journal of Consumer Research*, **17** (March): 454–62.

Hertel, G., Niedner, S. and Hermann, S. (2003), 'Motivation of software developers in open source projects: an internet-based survey of contributors to the Linux kernel', *Research Policy*, **32**: 1159–77.

Hildreth, P.M. (2004), *Going Virtual: Distributed Communities of Practice*, Hershey, PA: Idea Publishing Group.

Hoffman, D.L. and Novak, T.P. (1996), 'Marketing in hypermedia computer-mediated environments: conceptual foundations', *Journal of Marketing*, **60** (4): 50–68.

Holland, J.H. (1975), *Adaptation in Natural and Artificial Systems*, Ann Arbor, MI: University of Michigan Press.

Holland, J. and Baker, S.M. (2001), 'Customer participation in creating site brand loyalty', *Journal of Interactive Marketing*, **15** (4): 34–46.

Hoopes, D.G. and Postrel, S. (1999), 'Shared knowledge, "glitches", and product development performance', *Strategic Management Journal*, **20**: 837–65.

House, C.H. and Price, R.L. (1991), 'The return map: tracking product teams', *Harvard Business Review*, Jan–Feb: 92–100.

Iacobucci, D. and Ostrom, A. (1996), 'Commercial and interpersonal relationships. Using the structure of interpersonal relationships to understand individual-to-individual, individual-to-firm, and firm-to-firm relationships in commerce', *International Journal of Research in Marketing*, **13**: 53–72.

Iannacci, F. (2002), 'The economics of open source networks', MIT Working Paper, Cambridge, MA.

Iansiti, M. (1995), 'Technology integration: managing technological evolution in a complex environment', *Research Policy*, **24**: 521–42.

Iansiti, M. (1997), *Technology Integration: Making Critical Choices in a Dynamic World*, Boston, MA: Harvard Business School Press.

Iansiti, M. and Levien, R. (2004), 'Strategy as ecology', *Harvard Business Review*, March: 68–78.

Iansiti, M. and MacCormack, A. (1997), 'Developing products on Internet time', *Harvard Business Review*, September–October: 108–17.

Imai, K., Nonaka, I. and Takeuchi, H. (1985), 'Managing the new product development process: how Japanese companies learn and unlearn', in R.H. Hayes, K. Clark and C. Lorenz (eds), *The Uneasy Alliance: Managing the Productivity Technology Dilemma*, Boston, MA: Harvard Business School Press, pp. 337–76.

Jessor, R., Colby, A. and Shweder, R. (1996), *Ethnography and Human Development*, Chicago, IL: University of Chicago Press.

Johnson Brown, J. and Reingen, P.H. (1987), 'Social ties and word-of-mouth referral behavior', *Journal of Consumer Research*, **14** (December): 350–62.

Jones, Q. (1997), 'Virtual communities, virtual settlements and cyber-archeology: a theoretical outline', *Journal of Computer-Mediated Communication*, **3** (3), http://www.ascusc.org/jcmc/vol3/issue3/jones.html.

Jorgensen, D. (1989), *Participant Observation*, Newbury Park, CA: Sage.

Jurvetson, S. (2000), 'Turning customers into a sales force', *Business2.0*, March.

Kalyanaram, G. and Krishnan, V.V. (1997), 'Deliberate product definition: customizing the product definition process', *Journal of Marketing Research*, **34**: 276–85.

Kambil, A., Nunes, P.F. and Wilson, D. (1999), 'Transforming the marketspace with all-in-one markets', *International Journal of Electronic Commerce*, **3** (4), Summer: 11–28.

Kenny, D. and Marshall, J.F. (2000), 'Contextual marketing: the real business of the Internet', *Harvard Business Review*, **78** (6): 119–25.

Kim, A.J. (2000), *Community Building on the Web: Secret Strategies for Successful Online Communities*, Berkeley, CA: Peachpit Press.

Koch, S. and Schneider, G. (2002), 'Effort, co-operation, and co-ordination in an open source software project: GNOME', *Information Systems Journal*, **12** (1): 27–42.

Kogut, B. and Metiu, A. (2001), 'Open-source software development and distributed innovation', *Oxford Review of Economic Policy*, **17** (2): 248–64.

Kohli, A.K. and Jaworsky, B.J. (1990), 'Market orientation: the construct, research proposition, and managerial implications', *Journal of Marketing*, **54**: 1–18.

Kollock, P. (1999), 'The economies of online cooperation: gifts and public goods in computer communities', in M. Smith and P. Kollock (eds), *Communities in Cyberspace*, London: Routledge, pp. 3–25.

Kozinets, R.V. (1998), 'On netnography: initial reflections on consumer research investigations of cyberspace', *Advances in Consumer Research*, **25**: 366–71.

Kozinets, R.V. (1999), 'E-tribalized marketing? The strategic implications of virtual communities of consumption', *European Management Journal*, **17** (3): 252–64.

Kozinets, R.V. (2001), 'Utopian enterprise: articulating the meanings of Star Trek's culture of consumption', *Journal of Consumer Research*, **28** (June): 67–88.

Kozinets, R.V. (2002), 'The field behind the screen: using netnography for marketing research in online communities', *Journal of Marketing Research*, **39** (February): 61–72.

Kozinets, R.V. and Handelman, J.M. (1998), 'Ensouling consumption: a netnographic exploration of boycotting behavior', in J. Alba and W. Hutchinson (eds), *Advances in Consumer Research*, Provo, UT: Association for Consumer Research, vol. 25, pp. 475–80.

Kramer, R. (1991), 'Intergroup relations and organizational dilemmas: the role of categorization process', in L. Cummings and B. Staw (eds), *Research in Organizational Behavior*, Greenwich, CT: JAI Press, **13**, 191–228.

Krishnan, V.V. and Bhattacharya, S. (1998), 'The role of design flexibility in defining products under technological uncertainty', Working Paper, University of Austin at Texas, October.

Krishnan, V.V. and Ulrich, K. (2001), 'Product development decisions: a review of the literature', *Management Science*, **47** (1): 1–21.

Kumar, V. and Venkatesan, R. (2005), 'Who are the multichannel shoppers and how do they perform? Correlates of multichannel shopping behavior', *Journal of Interactive Marketing*, **19** (2): 44–62.

Kumar, N., Stern, L.W. and Anderson, J.C. (1993), 'Conducting interorganization research using key informants', *Academy of Management Journal*, **36** (6): 1633–51.

Laing, A., Hogg, G. and Newholm, T. (2004), 'Talking together: consumer communities and health care', *Advances in Consumer Research*, **31**: 67–73.

Lakhani, K. and von Hippel, E. (2000), 'How open source software works: "free" user-to-user assistance', Working Paper 4117, MIT Sloan School of Management.

Lakhani, K. and von Hippel, E. (2003), 'How open source software works: "free" user-to-user assistance', *Research Policy*, **32** (6): 923–43.

Langlois, R.N. and Robertson, P.L. (1995), *Firms, Markets and Economic Change: A Dynamic Theory of Business Institutions*, London: Routledge.

Lave, J. and Wenger, E. (1991), *Situated Learning*, Cambridge, MA: Cambridge University Press.

Lee, G.K. and Cole, R.E. (2000), 'The Linux kernel development as a model of knowledge creation', paper presented at the 20th Annual International Conference of the Strategic Management Society, Vancouver, October.

Lengnick-Hall, C.A. (1996), 'Customer contributions to quality: a different view of the customer-oriented firm', *Academy of Management Review*, **21** (3): 791–824.

Leonard, D. and Sensiper, S. (1998), 'The role of tacit knowledge in group innovation', *California Management Review*, **40** (3): 112–32.

Leonard, D. and Swap, W. (1999), *When Sparks Fly: Igniting Creativity in Groups*, Boston, MA: Harvard Business School Press.

Leonard-Barton, D. (1992), 'Core capabilities and core rigidities: a paradox in managing new product development', *Strategic Management Journal*, **13**: 111–25.

Leonard-Barton, D. (1995), *Wellsprings of Knowledge: Building and Sustaining the Sources of Innovation*, Boston, MA: Harvard Business School Press.

Leonard-Barton, D. and Rayport, J.F. (1997), 'Spark innovation through empathic design', *Harvard Business Review*, November–December: 102–13.

Lerner, J. and Tirole, J. (2002), 'Some simple economics of open source', *Journal of Industrial Economics*, **50** (2): 197–234.

Lerner, J. and Tirole, J. (2005), 'The scope of Open Source licensing', *Journal of Law, Economics and Organization*, **21**: 20–56.

Levy, S. (1984), *Hackers*, New York: Doubleday.

Liechty, J., Ramaswamy, V. and Cohen, S. (2001), 'Choice-menus for mass customization: an experimental approach for analyzing customer demand with an application to a web-based information service', *Journal of Marketing Research*, **38** (2), May: 183–96.

Linder, J.C., Jarvenpaa, S.L. and Davenport, T.H. (2003), 'Toward an innovation sourcing strategy', *MIT Sloan Management Review*, **44** (4): 43–9.

Liu, G.Z. (1999), 'Virtual community presence in Internet relay chatting', *Journal of Computer-Mediated Communication*, **5** (1): http://www.ascusc.org/jcmc/vol5/issue1/liu.html.

Lovelock, C.H. and Young, R.F. (1979), 'Look to consumers to increase productivity', *Harvard Business Review*, **57** (May–June): 168–78.

Lynn, G., Morone, J. and Paulson, A. (1996), 'Marketing and discount innovation: the probe and learn process', *California Management Review*, **38** (3): 8–37.

MacCormack, A., Verganti, R. and Iansiti, M. (2001), 'Developing products on Internet time: the anatomy of a flexible development process', *Management Science*, **47** (1): 133–50.

Maes, P. (1999), 'Smart commerce: the future of intelligent agents in cyberspace', *Journal of Interactive Marketing*, **13** (3): 66–76.

Malerba, F. (2000), *Economia dell'innovazione*, Rome: Carocci.

March, J.G. (1991), 'How decisions happen in organizations', *Human Computer International*, 6.

Martin, C.L. and Clark, T. (1996), 'Networks of customer-to-customer relationships in marketing: conceptual foundations and implications', in D. Iacobucci (ed.), *Network in Marketing*, Thousand Oaks, CA: Sage, pp. 342–66.

Mauss, M. (1959), *The Gift: The Form and the Reason for Exchange in Archaic Societies*, London: Routledge.

McAfee, A. and Oliveau, F.X. (2002), 'Confronting the limits of networks', *MIT Sloan Management Review*, **43**: 85–7.

McAlexander, J.H., Schouten, J.W. and Koenig, H.F. (2002), 'Building brand community', *Journal of Marketing*, **66** (January): 38–54.

McCracken, G. (1990), 'Culture and consumer behavior: an anthropological perspective', *Journal of the Market Research Society*, **32** (1): 3–11.

McWilliam, G. (2000), 'Building stronger brands through online communities', *MIT Sloan Management Review*, Spring: 43–54.

Meyer, M.H. and Lopez, L. (1995), 'Technology strategy in a software products company', *Journal of Product Innovation Management*, **12** (4): 194–206.

Micelli, S. (2000), *Imprese, Reti e Comunità Virtuali*, Milan: Etas.

Micelli, S. and Prandelli, E. (2000), 'Net marketing: ripensare il consumatore nel mondo della Rete', *Economia & Management*, **4** (July): 57–70.

Miles, M.B. and Huberman, A.M. (1994), *Qualitative Data Analysis: An Expanded Sourcebook*, Thousand Oaks, CA: Sage.

Miller, M.S. and Drexler K.E. (1988), 'Markets and computation: agoric open systems', in B. Huberman (ed.), *The Ecology of Computation*, North-Holland: Elsevier Science, pp. 315–17.

Mills, P.K., Chase, R.B. and Margulies, N. (1983), 'Motivating the client/employee system as a service production strategy', *Academy of Management Review*, **8**: 301–10.

Mills, P.K. and Morris, J.H. (1986), 'Clients as "partial employees" of service organizations: role of development in client participation', *Academy of Management Review*, **11** (4): 726–35.

Mockus, A., Fielding, R.T. and Herbsleb, J. (2000) (eds), 'A case study of open source software development: the Apache server', in *Proceedings of the Twenty-Second International Conference on Software Engineering*, pp. 263–72.

Montoya-Weiss, M.M., Massey, A.P. and Clapper, D.L. (1998), 'On line focus groups: conceptual issues and a research tool', *European Journal of Marketing*, **32** (7/8): 713–23.

Moody, J. (2001), *Rebel Code: Linux and the Open Source Revolution*, New York: Persens.

Moon, J.Y. and Sproull, L. (2000), 'Essence of distributed work: the case of the Linux kernel', *First Monday*, **5** (11): http://www.firstmonday.dk/issues/issue5_11/moon/.

Moore, W. and Pessemier, E. (1993), *Product Planning and Management: Designing and Delivering Value*, New York: McGraw-Hill.

Muniz, A.M. and O'Guinn, T.C. (2001), 'Brand community', *Journal of Consumer Research*, **27** (March): 412–32.

Nahapiet, J. and Ghoshal, S. (1998), 'Social capital, intellectual capital, and the organizational advantage', *Academy of Management Review*, **23** (2): 242–66.

Nalebuff, B. and Ayres, I. (2003), *Why Not? How to use Everyday Ingenuity to Solve Problems*, Boston, MA: Harvard Business School Press.

Nambisan, S. (2002), 'Designing virtual customer environments for new product development: toward a theory', *Academy of Management Review*, **27** (3): 392–413.

Nelson, R.R. and Winter, S.G. (1982), *An Evolutionary Theory of Economic Change*, Cambridge, MA: Harvard University Press.

Nonaka, I. and Konno, N. (1998), 'The concept of "Ba": building a foundation for knowledge creation', *California Management Review*, **3**: 40–54.

Nonaka, I. and Takeuchi, H. (1995), *The Knowledge-creating Company*, Oxford and New York: Oxford University Press.

Nunamaker, J., Briggs, R.O., Mittleman, D., Vogél, D.R. and Balthazard, P.A. (1997), 'Lessons from a dozen years of group support systems research: a discussion of lab and field findings', *Journal of Management Information Systems*, **25**: 163–207.

O'Mahony, S. (2003), 'Guarding the Commons: how open source contributors protect their work', *Research Policy*, **32** (7): 1179–98.

Okleshen, C. and Grossbart, S. (1998), 'Usenet groups, virtual community and consumer behavior', in J.W. Alba and J.W. Hutchinson (eds), *Advances in Consumer Research*, Vol. 25, Provo, UT: Association for Consumer Research, pp. 276–82.

Olson, M. (1967), *The Logic of Collective Action*, Boston, MA: Harvard University Press.

Orlikowsky, W. (1992), 'The duality of technology: rethinking the concept of technology in organizations', *Organization Science*, **3** (3): 398–427.

Paccagnella, L. (1997), 'Getting the seats of your pants dirty: strategies for ethnographic research on virtual communities', *Journal of Computer-Mediated Communication*, **3** (1): http://jcmc.indiana.edu/vol3/issue1/paccagnella.html.

Pagani, M. (2003), *Multimedia and Interactive Digital TV: Managing the Opportunities Created by Digital Convergence*, IRM Press.

Park, C., Whan Jun, S. and MacInnis, D. (2000), 'Choosing what I want versus rejecting what I do not want: an application of decision framing to product option choice decisions', *Journal of Marketing Research*, **37** (2): 187–202.

Pavlicek, R. (1999), 'Keys to effective Linux advocacy within your organisation', http://users.crols.com/plavlicek/oreilly/als-fullpaper-1999.txt.

Peppers, D. and Rogers, M. (1997), *Enterprise One to One*, New York: Currency.

Perens, B. (1999), 'The open source definition', in Di Bona et al. (eds), pp. 171–88.

Peterson, R.A. (1995), 'Relationship marketing and the consumer', *Journal of the Academy of Marketing Science*, **23** (4): 278–81.

Pettigrew, A. (1990), 'Longitudinal field research on change: theory and practice', *Organizational Science*, **3**: 267–92.

Philipps, L.W. (1981), 'Assessing measurement error in key informant reports: a methodological note on organizational analysis in marketing', *Journal of Marketing Research*, **18** (November): 395–415.

Piller, F., Ihl. C., Fuller, J. and Stotko, C. (2004), 'Toolkits for open innovation – the case of mobile phone games', in *Proceedings of the 37th Hawaii International Conference on System Sciences*, 5–8 January.

Porter, M.E. (2001), 'Strategy and the Internet', *Harvard Business Review*, **79** (3): 63–79.

Postmes, T., Spears, R. and Lea, M. (1999), 'Social idendity, normative content and deindividuation', in N. Ellemers, R. Spears and B. Doosje (eds), *Social Identity*, Oxford: Blackwell: 164–83.

Powell, W.W., Koput, K.W. and Smith-Doerr, L. (1996), 'Interorganizational collaboration and the locus of innovation: networks of learning in biotechnology', *Administrative Science Quarterly*, **41** (2): 116–45.

Prahalad, C.K. and Krishnan, M.S. (2002), 'The dynamic synchronization of strategy and Information Technology', *MIT Sloan Management Review*, **43** (4): 24.

Prahalad, C.K. and Ramaswamy, V. (2000), 'Co-opting customer competence', *Harvard Business Review*, **88** (3): 79–87.

Prahalad, C.K. and Ramaswamy, V. (2003), 'The new frontier of experience innovation', *MIT Sloan Management Review*, **44** (4): 12–18.

Prahalad, C.K. and Ramaswamy, V. (2004), 'Co-creation experiences: the new practice in value creation', *Journal of Interactive Marketing*, **18** (3): 5–14.

Prandelli, E. and Verona, G. (2006), *Marketing in Rete. Oltre Internet verso il Nuovo Marketing*, Milan: McGraw-Hill.

Prandelli, E., Sawhney, M. and Verona, G. (2006a), 'The emerging organizational models of distributed innovation: towards a taxonomy', in B. Renzl, K. Matzler and H. Hinterhuber (eds), *The Future of Knowledge Management*, New York: Palgrave, pp. 137–60.

Prandelli, E., Verona, G. and Raccagni, D. (2006b), 'Diffusion of web-based product innovation', *California Management Review*, **40** (4), Summer: 109–35.

Prandelli, E. and von Krogh, G. (2000), 'Fare leverage sulla conoscenza tacita dei consumatori: verso una nuova economia cognitiva', *Sinergie*, **51**: 49–84.

Prelec, D. (2000), 'The information pump', Working Paper, Center for Innovation in Product Development, MIT, Cambridge, MA.

Quinn, J.B. (1985), 'Managing innovation: controlled chaos', *Harvard Business Review*, May–June: 73–84.

Quinn, J.B., Anderson, P. and Finkelstein, S. (1996), 'Leveraging intellect', *Academy of Management Executives*, **10** (3): 7–27.

Rammert, W. (2002), 'The cultural shaping of technologies and the politics of technodiversity', in K.H. Sörensen and R. Williams (eds), *Shaping Technology, Guiding Policy: Concepts, Spaces and Tools*, Cheltenham: Edward Elgar, 173–94.

Randall, T., Terwiesch, C. and Ulrich, K.T. (2007), 'User design of customized product', *Marketing Science*, **26**: 268–80.

Rangaswamy, A. and van Bruggen, G.H. (2005), 'Opportunities and challenges in multichannel marketing: an introduction to the Special Issue', *Journal of Interactive Marketing*, **19** (2): 5–11.

Raymond, E.S. (1999), 'Linux and open-source success', *IEEE Software*, **16** (1): 85–9.

Raymond, E.S. (2001), *The Cathedral and the Bazaar: Musings on Linux and Open Source by an Accidental Revolutionary*, Sebastopol, CA: O'Reilly.

Reichheld, F. and Schefter, P. (2000), 'E-Loyalty', *Harvard Business Review*, July–August: 105–13.

Reid, E.M. (1999), 'Hierarchy and power: social control in cyberspace', in M.A. Smith and P. Kollock (eds), *Communities in Cyberspace*, London: Routledge, pp. 107–34.

Rheingold, H. (1993), *The Virtual Community: Homesteading on the Electronic Frontier*, Reading, MA: Addison-Wesley.

Rogers, E. (1995), *Diffusion of Innovation*, 4th edn, New York: Free Press.

Rothaermel, F.T. and Sugiyama, S. (2001), 'Virtual Internet communities and commercial success: individual and community-level theory grounded in the atypical case of TimeZone.com', *Journal of Management*, **27** (3): 297–312.

Ruefli, T.W., Whinston, A. and Wiggins, R.R. (2001), 'The digital technological environment', in J. Wind and V. Mahajan (eds), *Digital Marketing*, New York: Wiley, pp. 26–58.

Rullani, E. (1997), 'Tecnologie che Generano Valore: Divisione del Lavoro Cognitivo e Rivoluzione Digitale', *Economia e Politica Industriale*, **93**: 5–17.

Sawhney, M. and Kotler, P. (2001), 'Marketing in the age of information democracy', in D. Iacobucci (ed.), *Kellogg on Marketing*, Chicago, IL: John Wiley, pp. 368–408.

Sawhney, M. and Parikh, D. (2001), 'Where value lives in a networked world', *Harvard Business Review*, January: 79–86.

Sawhney, M. and Prandelli, E. (2000a), 'Communities of creation: managing distributed innovation in turbulent markets', *California Management Review*, **42** (4): 24–54.

Sawhney, M. and Prandelli, E. (2000b), 'Beyond customer knowledge management: customers as knowledge co-creators', in J. Malhotra (ed.), *Knowledge Management and Virtual Organizations*, Hershey, PA: Idea Group Publishing, pp. 258–81.

Sawhney, M., Prandelli, E. and Verona, G. (2003), 'The power of innomediation', *MIT Sloan Management Review*, **44** (2): 77–82.

Sawhney, M., Verona, G. and Prandelli, E. (2005), 'Collaborating to create: the Internet as a platform for customer engagement in product innovation', *Journal of Interactive Marketing*, **19** (4): 4–17.

Schmitt, F.F. (1994), *Socializing Epistemology: The Social Dimensions of Knowledge*, Boston, MA: Rowman & Littlefield.

Schneider, B. and Bowen, D.E. (1995), *Winning the Service Game*, Boston, MA: Harvard Business School Press.

Schumpeter, J. (1991 [1934]), *The Theory of Economic Development: An Inquiry into Profits, Capital, Credit, Interest and the Business Cycle*, New York: Oxford University Press.

Schumpeter, J. (1943), *Capitalism, Socialism and Democracy*, London: Allen & Unwin.

Shan, W., Walker, G. and Kogut, B. (1994), 'Interfirm cooperation and startup innovation in the biotechnology industry', *Strategic Management Journal*, **15** (3): 387–94.

Shankar, V., Smith, A.K. and Rangaswamy, A. (2003), 'Customer satisfaction and loyalty in online and offline environments', *International Journal of Research in Marketing*, **20**: 153–75.

Shapiro, B.P. (1989), 'What the hell is market oriented?', *Harvard Business Review*, **66** (November–December): 119–25.

Shapiro, C. and Varian, H.L. (1998), *Information Rules: A Strategic Guide to the Network Economy*, Boston, MA: Harvard Business School Press.

Sherry, J.F. (1995), *Contemporary Marketing and Consumer Behavior: An Anthropological Sourcebook*, Thousand Oaks, CA: Sage.

Sherry, J.F. and Kozinets, R.V. (2001), 'Qualitative inquiry in marketing and consumer research', in D. Iacobucci (ed.), *Kellogg on Marketing*, New York: John Wiley, pp. 165–94.

Sommers, W.P. (1982), 'Product development: new approachess in the 1980's', in M.L. Tushman and W.L. Moore (eds), *Readings in the Management of Innovation*, Marshfield, MA: Pitman, pp. 51–9.

Spencer, W.J. (1990), 'Research to product: a major U.S. challenge', *California Management Review*, **32** (2): 35–53.

Spender, J.C. (1996), 'Making knowledge the basis of a dynamic theory of the firm', *Strategic Management Journal*, **17**: 45–62.

Sproull, L. and Kiesler, S. (1986), 'Reducing social context cues: electronic mail in organizational communication', *Management Science*, **23** (11): 1492–512.

Sproull, L. and Kiesler, S. (1991), *Connections: New Ways of Working in the Networked Organization*, Cambridge, MA: MIT Press.

Srinivasan, V. 'Seenu', Lovejoy, W.S. and Beach, D. (1997), 'Integrated product design for marketability and manufacturing', *Journal of Marketing Research*, **34**: 154–63.

Stallman, R. (1984), 'The GNU manifesto', http://www.gnu.org/gnu/manifesto.html.

Sutton, R. (2002), 'Weird ideas that spark innovation', *Sloan Management Review*, **43** (2), Winter: 83–7.

Szulanski, G. (1996), 'Exploring internal stickiness: impediments to the transfer of best practice within the firm', *Strategic Management Journal*, **17**: 27–43.

Tabrizi, B. and Walleigh, R. (1997), 'Defining next generation products: an inside look', *Harvard Business Review*, **75** (6): 116–24.

Teece, D.J., Pisano, G. and Shuen, A. (1997), 'Dynamic capabilities and strategic management', *Strategic Management Journal*, **18** (7): 509–33.

Thomke, S.H. (1998), 'Managing experimentation in the design of new products', *Management Science*, **44** (6): 743–62.

Thomke, S. and Kuemmerle, W. (2002), 'Asset accumulation, interdependence and technological change: evidence from pharmaceutical drug discovery', *Strategic Management Journal*, **23** (7): 619–35.

Thomke, S. and von Hippel, E. (2002), 'Customers as innovators: a new way to create value', *Harvard Business Review*, **80** (4): 74–81.

Thomke, S.H., von Hippel, E.A. and Franke, R.R. (1998), 'Modes of experimentation: an innovation process – and competitive – variable', *Research Policy*, **27**: 315–32.

Thurow, L.C. (1997), 'Needed: a new system of intellectual property rights', *Harvard Business Review*, September–October: 94–103.

Tidd, J., Bessant, J. and Pavitt, K. (2001), *Managing Innovation*, 2nd edn, Englewood Cliffs, NJ: Prentice-Hall.

Torvalds, L. and Diamond, D. (2001), *Just for Fun: The Story of an Accidental Revolution*, New York: Harper Business.

Toubia, O. (2004), 'Idea generation, creativity, and incentives', Working Paper, Massachusetts Institute of Technology, January.

Troilo, G. (2001), *Marketing Knowledge Management*, Milan: McGraw-Hill.

Tushman, M.C. and O'Really, C.A. (1997), *Winning Through Innovation: A Practical Guide to Leading Organizational Change and Renewal*, Boston, MA: Harvard Business School Press.

Tyre, M.J. and von Hippel, E. (1997), 'The situated nature of adaptive learning in organizations', *Organization Science*, **8** (1): 71–83.

Ulrich, K.T. and Eppinger, S.D. (1999), *Product Design and Development*, New York: McGraw-Hill.

Upton, D.M. and McAfee, A. (1996), 'The real virtual factory', *Harvard Business Review*, July–August: 123–33.

Urban, G.L. (2000), 'Listening in to customer dialogues on the web', Working paper, Center for Innovation in Product Development, Cambridge, MA, MIT.

Urban, G.L. and Hauser, J.R. (1993), *Design and Marketing of New Products*, Englewood Cliffs, NJ: Prentice-Hall.

Urban, G.L. and Hauser, J.R. (2002), 'Listening in to find unmet customer needs and solutions', Working Paper 156, Center for eBusiness, MIT, July.

Urban, G.L., Sultan, F. and Qualls, W.J. (2000), 'Making trust the center of your Internet strategy', *Sloan Management Review*, Fall (1): 39–48.

Urban, G. and von Hippel, E. (1988), 'Lead user analysis for the development of new industrial products', *Management Science*, **34** (5), May: 569–82.

Urban, G., Weinberg, B. and Hauser, J. (1996), 'Premarket forecasting of really-new products', *Journal of Marketing*, **60**: 47–60.

Verona, G. (1999), 'A resource-based view of product development', *Academy of Management Review*, **24** (1): 132–42.

Verona, G. and Prandelli, E. (2002), 'A dynamic model of customer loyalty to sustain competitive advantage on the Web', *European Management Journal*, **20** (3): 299–309.

Verona, G., Prandelli, E. and Sawhney, M. (2006), 'Innovation and virtual environments: towards virtual knowledge brokers', *Organization Studies*, **27** (6): 765–88.

Vicari, S. (2001), 'Il management della virtualità', in Vicari (ed.), *Economia della Virtualità*, Milan: Egea, pp. 5–60.

Vixie, P. (1999), 'Software engineering', in Di Bona et al. (eds), pp. 91–100.

von Hippel, E. (1977), 'Has a customer already developed your next product?', *Sloan Management Review*, **18** (2), Winter: 73–4.

von Hippel, E. (1986), 'Lead users: a source of novel product concepts', *Management Science*, **32** (7): 791–805.

von Hippel, E. (1988), *The Sources of Innovation*, Oxford: Oxford University Press.

von Hippel, E. (1994), ' "Sticky information" and the locus of problem solving: implications for innovation', *Management Science*, **40** (4): 429–39.

von Hippel, E. (1998), 'Economics of product development by users: the impact of "sticky" local information', *Management Science*, **5**: 629–44.

von Hippel, E. (2001a), 'Perspective: user toolkits for innovation', *Journal of Product Innovation Management*, **18**: 247–57.

von Hippel, E. (2001b), 'User toolkits for innovation', *Journal of Product Innovation Management*, **18** (4), July: 247–57.

von Hippel, E. (2005), *Democratizing Innovation*, Cambridge, MA: MIT Press.

von Hippel, E. and Katz, R. (2002), 'Shifting innovation to users via toolkits', *Management Science*, **48** (7): 821–33.

von Hippel, E. and von Krogh, G. (2003), 'Exploring the open source software phenomenon: issues for organization science', *Organization Science*, **14** (2): 209–23.

von Krogh, G. (2003), 'Open-source software development', *MIT Sloan Management Review*, Spring: 14–18.

von Krogh, G. and Roos, J. (1995), *Organizational Epistemology*, New York: St. Martin's Press.

von Krogh, G., Spaeth, S. and Lakhani, K. (2003), 'Community, joining, and specialization in open-source software innovation: a case study', *Research Policy*, **32** (7): 1217–41.

von Krogh, G. and von Hippel, E. (2003), Special issue on open source software development, *Research Policy*, **2**.

Wallace, P. (1999), *The Psychology of the Internet*, Cambridge: Cambridge University Press.

Walther, J.B. (1992), 'Interpersonal effects in computer-mediated interaction: a relational perspective', *Communication Research*, **19** (1): 52–90.

Walther, J.B. (1995), 'Relational aspects of computer-mediated communication: experimental observations over time', *Organization Science*, **6**: 186–203.

Warisse Turner, J., Grube, J.A. and Meyers, J. (2001), 'Developing an optimal match within online communities: an exploration of CMC support communities and traditional support', *Journal of Communication*, June: 231–51.

Watson, N. (1997), 'Why we argue about virtual community: a case study of the Phish.Net Fan community', in S.G. Jones (ed.), *Virtual Culture: Identity and Communication in Cybersociety*, Thousand Oaks, CA: Sage, pp. 102–33.

Wayland, R.E. and Cole, P.M. (1997), *Customer Connections*, Boston, MA: Harvard Business School Press.

Weissman, R.X. (1998), 'Online or off target?', *American Demographics*, **20** (11): 20–21.

Wellman, B. and Gulia, M. (1999), 'Virtual communities as communities: net surfers don't ride alone', in M.A. Smith and P. Kollock (eds), *Communities in Cyberspace*, London: Routledge, pp. 167–95.

Wenger, E. (1998), *Communities of Practice: Learning, Meaning, and Identity*, Cambridge: Cambridge University Press.

Wenger, E. and Snyder, W.M. (2000), Communities of practice: the organizational frontier', *Harvard Business Rewiew*, January–February: 139–45.

Wheeler, D. (2002), 'Why open source software/free software (OSS/FS)? Look at the numbers!', Working Paper, http://www.dwheeler.com/oss_fs_why.html.

Wheelwright, S. and Clark, K.B. (1992), 'Creating project plans to focus product development', *Harvard Business Review*, March–April: 71–82.

Wikström, S. (1996), 'The customer as co-producer', *European Journal of Marketing*, **30** (4): 6–19.

Williamson, O.E. (1985), *The Economic Institutions of Capitalism*, New York: Free Press.

Wind, J. and Rangaswamy, A. (2001), 'Customerization: the next revolution in mass customization', *Journal of Interactive Marketing*, **15** (1): 13–45.

Youngblood, M.D. (1997), 'Leadership at the edge of chaos: from control to creativity', *Planning Review*, **5**: 8–14.

Zahra, S.A. and George, G. (2002), 'Absorptive capacity: a review, reconceptualization and extension', *Academy of Management Review*, **27** (2): 189–203.

Zajac, E. and Olsen, C. (1993), 'From transaction costs to transactional value analysis: implications for the study of interorganizational strategies', *Journal of Management Studies*, **30**: 131–44.

Zaltman, G. (1997), 'Rethinking market research: putting people back', *Journal of Marketing Research*, **34** (November): 424–37.

Zaltman, G. and Higie, R.A. (1993), 'Seeing the voice of the customer: the Zaltman metaphor elicitation technique', Report Number 93–114, Marketing Science Institute, Cambridge, MA.

Index